REFUGE DENIED:

Problems in the Protection

of Vietnamese and Cambodians in Thailand

and the Admission of Indochinese Refugees

into the United States

The Lawyers Committee for Human Rights

Since 1978 the Lawyers Committee has served as a public interest law center. The Lawyers Committee works to promote international human rights law and legal procedures in the United States and abroad. The chairman of the Lawyers Committee is Marvin Frankel; Michael Posner is its Executive Director; Arthur Helton is director of the Committee's Political Asylum Project.

Bound copies of this report are available from:

Lawyers Committee for Human Rights
330 Seventh Avenue
New York, New York 10001

TABLE OF CONTENTS

PREFACE

This report describes the continuing plight of Cambodian[1] and Vietnamese asylum seekers[2] in Thailand as well as issues relating to refugee processing in the United States (U.S.). The report is an update of two prior reports by the Lawyers Committee for Human Rights. *After The Worst* (1985) described the human rights situation in Cambodia six years after the Vietnamese invasion of that country and the consequent fall from power of the murderous Khmer Rouge under Pol Pot. *Seeking Shelter* (1987) described the protection problems of the nearly 300,000 Cambodians along the Thai-Cambodian border. That 1987 report found that the Cambodians faced daily risks to life and physical security from a myriad of sources, including those from whom they had fled, their guards in Thailand, and even each other -- all without effective protection or the possibility of meaningful legal redress.

In January and September-October 1988, the Lawyers Committee sent missions to assess the current situation of Cambodians in Thailand and expanded the inquiry to assess refugee protection and U.S. admissions procedures, not only for Cambodians but also for Vietnamese and Laotians.[3] Arthur C. Helton, Director of the Lawyers Committee's Political Asylum Project, led the missions. In January, he was accompanied by Al Santoli, an author, and Lawrence J. Eisenstein, a lawyer at the firm of Covington & Burling in Washington, D.C. In October, Mr. Helton was accompanied again by Mr. Santoli, and by Roni Rubenstein, a member of the New York State Bar. During the course of these missions of inquiry, representatives of the Lawyers Committee interviewed well over 100 asylum seekers and numerous governmental and non-governmental representatives. The expanded scope of the inquiry sought to address concerns raised by the Lawyers Committee's previous work with asylum seekers in Thailand. Those interviewed by the Lawyers Committee for this report included: Somphorn Klingpongsa and Prapakorn Smiti of the Ministry of the Interior and Kobsak Chutikul and Kasit Phirom of the Ministry of Foreign Affairs of the Royal Thai Government; Special Col. Sanan Kajornklam, Special Col.

---

[1] For reasons solely of convenience for the reader, the terms "Cambodia," "Cambodians," or "Khmer" are use throughout this report. No political point is implied, nor should any be inferred, by the use of these terms.

[2] The term "asylum seeker" is used generally in the protection section of this report instead of the term "refugee" which has a specific legal meaning under the 1951 Convention and 1967 Protocol relating to the Status of Refugees.

[3] A separate report on the protection of Laotian asylum seekers in Thailand is in preparation.

Somsak Srisupundit and Col. Hath Wirasamrith of the Royal Thai Army; U.S. Ambassador Dan O'Donohue and Messrs. Bruce Beardsley and Alan Jury of the U.S. Embassy; Pierre Jambor of the office of the United Nations High Commissioner for Refugees (UNHCR); Robert Burrows of the United Nations Border Relief Organization (UNBRO); Urs Boeqli of the International Committee of the Red Cross (ICRC); Jim Anderson of the International Rescue Committee; David Belskis of Save The Children; Bob Medrala of the American Refugee Committee; and Susan Walker of Operation Handicap International.

An earlier draft of this report was submitted to the Thai government in October 1988, and formed the basis of discussions with government officials from Thailand and the U.S., as well as with representatives of international organizations and voluntary agencies. The report has been revised and updated to reflect those discussions. Some who were interviewed requested that they not be identified in this report because of the sensitive nature of the matters they disclosed to the Lawyers Committee, and those requests have been honored.

The principal authors of this report are Al Santoli and Lawrence J. Eisenstein. Roni Rubenstein and Arthur C. Helton are contributing authors and edited the report.[4]

---

[4] In the course of preparing for the missions and the report, assistance was provided by the following persons: James Anderson, Michael Brady, Ilana Eden, Annette Harris, Julie Lynch, Jennifer Meyerhardt and Suzanne Unger.

I. INTRODUCTION

Since 1975, brutal wars and repressive governments have forced approximately two million Cambodians, Lao and Vietnamese to flee their homelands. By foot and by boat they have traveled to Thailand, and other countries in the region, including Hong Kong and Malaysia. Most went to Thailand where more than 380,000 people remain today. The Thai government has vacillated in its response to these arrivals, at times reacting with apparent compassion, and at other times reacting with callousness and abuse. This report examines the current treatment of Cambodians and Vietnamese in Thailand. The report also analyses the U.S. overseas admissions procedure for asylum seekers in Thailand. Recommendations are made to enhance the legal protection of asylum seekers in Thailand and fairness in U.S. refugee processing.

Fourteen years after the fall of Saigon and Phnom Penh the flow of refugees from these countries continues. The first to leave South Vietnam after the government surrendered to the North Vietnamese Army on April 30, 1975, were those associated with the former regime, who were dealt with harshly. Deteriorating civil liberties at home, food shortages, drought, floods, and the desire to avoid military service led to the flight of members of the middle class and the peasantry. In 1978, Hanoi set out to abolish all trade and private business enterprise. The government closed businesses, especially those owned by ethnic Chinese, ordered owners to return to their villages or move to "new economic zones." The country was to be rid of "undesirables." The massive exodus had begun. By 1979, approximately 600,000, Vietnamese, many of whom were ethnic Chinese, had left, many going to Thailand. Most were ultimately resettled in the U.S.

In late 1978, Vietnam invaded Cambodia, which had been devastated by the brutal Khmer Rouge regime under Pol Pot. Since the Khmer Rouge had overrun Phnom Penh in 1975 and established Democratic Kampuchea, the regime had carried out a policy of eliminating all real and imagined opponents. Forced evacuations of the capital and a regime of forced labor imposed on a populace weakened by avoidable starvation and treatable diseases took an even greater toll. Before the Vietnamese army routed Pol Pot's regime, over a million of the country's total population of seven million may have perished. To escape the mass killing and, later, the Vietnamese invasion, scores of thousands of Cambodians fled the country overland to Thailand. As a result of its prior investigations, in 1987 the Lawyers Committee reported the following findings and recommendations:

1.Because of threats to physical security posed by proximity to the border, the Lawyers Committee

3

recommended that the camps be moved farther away from the border, and that the approximately 24,000 Cambodians in Khao I Dang camp not be returned to the border.

2. Because of attacks by bandits, the Committee urged Thailand to firmly exercise its law enforcement responsibilities along the border.

3. Because of abuses by the Thai rangers who guard the camps, the Committee supported proposals for reform being considered by the Thai authorities concerning recruitment, training and discipline of the guards.

4. Because of concerns about the Khmer Rouge control forces of some 59,000 Cambodians living in camps, the Committee urged Thailand to assist in enforcing the freedom of those Cambodians to move to other camps.

5. Because of protection problems on the border, the Committee recommended that the mandate of the UNHCR be extended to the Cambodians on the border.

Today, approximately 330,000 Cambodians remain in Thai border camps waiting for resettlement abroad or a political settlement that would permit them to return to Cambodia. Conditions are inhumane. They live in closed border camps, are exposed to cross-border conflict and are victimized by criminals without effective redress or protection.

In response to concerns raised by the international community, the Thai authorities have deployed a new DPPU to take the place of the infamous Task Force 80 rangers, whose abuses of Cambodians were the subject of the Committee's 1987 report. The deployment of the DPPU has helped to diminish abuses of Cambodians and Vietnamese by Thai guards. Much remains to be done, however, to insure the basic safety and physical security of the Cambodians.

Perhaps the most dramatic development in the region occurred in January 1988 with the announcement by the Thai government of a policy to push-back Vietnamese "boat people" arriving on the southern and eastern coasts of Thailand. A reaction to increased arrivals of boat people, the Thai policy produced much suffering and carnage. While precise figures are unavailable, hundreds have drowned. Push-backs involved Thai police as well as fishermen, some of whom had been deputized by the government. Even United Nations (U.N.) anti-piracy resources may have been used to further

4

this brutal policy. While the central Thai government publicly withdrew from this controversial policy shortly after its inception, push-backs are still routinely occurring on the coasts. The Thai authorities have limited or denied access to the UNHCR to assess the dimension of the problem and ensure the protection of those arriving.

The hostility toward asylum seekers in Southeast Asia escalated dramatically in 1988. The hostility has spread as the governments of Thailand, Hong Kong and Malaysia have engaged in a grim competition to shift the burden elsewhere. The recent Thai push-back policy has caused a sharp increase in piracy. Pirates are encouraged to attack defenseless boat people by abusive push-back policies or practices. Thailand and other governments in the region say they are willing only to grant "first" (or temporary) asylum, depending on western countries to take those who are made available for resettlement. Indeed, since 1975, the U.S. has resettled over 800,000 Vietnamese, Laotians and Cambodians.

Many have been denied resettlement, however, never learning the reasons for such denials or being given an opportunity for effective appeal or review. From the perspective of the individual refugee status applicant, the U.S. processing procedure appears arbitrary and capricious. The most controversial recent example is the over 10,000 Cambodians at Khao I Dang camp who have been denied resettlement in the U.S. on account of alleged affiliation with the Khmer Rouge. In any event, a nation's obligation to provide humanitarian protection is in no respect dependent on another country's refugee or immigration policy, including resettlement abroad. Rather, it is an independent human rights principle. There is no easy short-term solution to the current asylum crisis in Southeast Asia, which will require a considerable effort on the part of all the parties to work together to find solutions. But in the search for stability and solution, the fundamental human rights of those in the camps must not be ignored. They should not be subject to arbitrary confinement or rejection at the shore, and pirates or others who abuse them should be brought to justice. Such firm intervention is required in order to begin the rescue of asylum in Southeast Asia.

II. PRINCIPAL PROTECTION CONCLUSIONS AND RECOMMENDATIONS

1. Thailand's policy of pushing back and preventing Vietnamese boat people from landing on Thai shores represents a serious violation of human rights and humanitarian principles. The right not to be returned to a territory where there is a risk of persecution is a fundamental precept of refugee law and includes a right not to be rejected at a border or shore. The spate of rammings and shootings by Thai security officials, including Thai naval and marine police, have resulted in hundreds of deaths of Vietnamese boat people.

2. The push-back policy has also inspired a rash of piracy incidents, unmitigated in their violence and cruelty. Hundreds of Vietnamese have been raped, robbed and murdered by Thai fisherman. In addition, Thailand's refusal to allow Vietnamese boat people to disembark from freighters who have rescued them at sea is unacceptable. The Lawyers Committee urges that the Thai government ensure respect for the basic human rights of Vietnamese boat people. Thai police should take the necessary steps to curb piracy. In addition, the Lawyers Committee urges that respect for the obligation of vessels to rescue boat people in distress in international waters be encouraged.

3. An anti-piracy program in Thailand involving the governments of Thailand and the United States as well as the United Nations has severely deteriorated and should be enhanced in order to protect boat people from abuses and death. Reports that resources have been diverted from the program and even used to further the push-back policy should be carefully investigated. In order to better coordinate anti-piracy and protection efforts on both coasts and the islands, the Lawyers Committee recommends:

a) The Thai government should grant full access to the UNHCR and U.S. Embassy anti-piracy and protection officers to interview refugees immediately upon arrival in Thailand or the islands and coordinate and share information on piracy. Immediate access will facilitate the prosecution of offenders.

b) U.S. Embassy personnel should on a regular basis monitor Thailand's border and coastlines, and develop a system of reliable information contacts. Routine searches of the islands should be conducted and indigenous employees with multi-lingual capabilities need to be used.

c) The U.S. Embassy should identify a regular liaison to coordinate with Thai officials in Bangkok on a regular basis. This would provide the ability to respond to a developing or ongoing crisis through the communication of reports from field investigators.

4. The Lawyers Committee urges an end to Thailand's asylum deterrence policies. The enforcement of onerous living conditions as a means of discouraging others from fleeing persecution is unlawful and inhumane. Most refugees in Thailand reside in a political and legal limbo, physically confined and restricted in the development of the most fundamental economic, political and social structures.

The Lawyers Committee recommends that the Thai government take measures to improve living conditions in all camps, addressing such points as chronic overcrowding and mental health problems. Basic amenities should be made available to all camp residents without discrimination. The Lawyers Committee also supports the establishment of a more normal social community with formal educational and vocational programs and employment opportunities. In this regard, the sprawling Site 2, with its 170,000 inhabitants, could be divided into smaller enclaves.

5. Abuses of asylum seekers by Thai rangers who guard the border camps have been a serious problem in the past. Reports of such abuses have diminished over the last year. The Lawyers Committee supports the creation and full deployment of the recently established and specially-recruited and trained DPPU. The DPPU should continue to receive training and support from the U.N.

6. Cambodians living along the Thai-Cambodian border remain subject to violence and sexual abuse committed by other Cambodians, including KPNLF guerrillas, bandits and extortionists. Site 2 in particular is plagued by lawlessness, which is exacerbated by crowded living conditions and the growing despair of camp inhabitants. While the Thai government has been reluctant to enforce a legal code within the camp, asserting that it is the Front's primary responsibility to maintain law and order, the Lawyers Committee believes that it is essential that a system of law be brought to the camps. Criminals must be held responsible for abuses.

Accordingly, the Lawyers Committee urges the Thai government to recognize its responsibility to apply law within the camps under which individuals are held accountable for their actions. In the case of serious crimes committed on Thai soil, offenders should be apprehended, tried under Thai law and punished. A reliable dispute resolution mechanism should be established within the camps to deal with less serious offenses. In addition, corrupt camp officials and leaders should be effectively disciplined and, if warranted, removed.

7. While Thailand has granted the UNHCR 24-hour access in the Ban Thad camp, the Lawyers Committee urges that international organizations be permitted to have specialists on security present on a 24-hour basis in all camps in order to help assure protection of the inhabitants. These specialists could work in conjuction with the proposed UNBRO-DPPU liaison personnel.

8. The commingling of civilians and military personnel in camps along the Thai/Cambodian border, as well as the proximity of the Cambodian settlements in Thailand to the border, continues to pose a serious and often deadly threat to the safety of their inhabitants. All of the Cambodian camps are within six miles of the Thai-Cambodian border; indeed, Site 2, which houses approximately 170,000 individuals, is within one mile of the border. The Lawyers Committee urges that civilians and military personnel be separated and that the integrity of civilian settlements be preserved and honored. Further, given the continuation of armed hostilities along the border, the Lawyers Committee continues to advocate that these settlements be moved further away from the border to ensure a minimum level of safety.[5]

9. While the Thai government has in the past refrained from relocating the inhabitants of Khao I Dang camp, it continues to assert its plans to force camp residents to relocate in border camps. The Lawyers Committee opposes the closing of Khao I Dang and is particularly concerned that these individuals' protection under the mandate of the UNHCR will be compromised as a result of such a move. In the event the Thai government does implement its decision

---

[5] Pending the movement of the settlements from the border area, the Lawyers Committee supports the adoption of interim measures to enhance the safety of the camps' inhabitants and to ensure an efficient evacuation in the event of armed hostilities. Security experts have recommended that evacuation sites be removed from artillery range; evacuation should be planned to ensure rapid and orderly movement in the event of attack; and within the camps, earthen bunkers around facilities such as schools, clinics and temples should be reinforced.

to relocate Khao I Dang, these individuals should not be moved near a border settlement such as Site 2, which is already overcrowded and unsafe. The Lawyers Committee continues to support the establishment of a separate site, a safe distance from the border, to house the residents of Khao I Dang under UNHCR protection and monitoring.

10. The Lawyers Committee is concerned with the status of unauthorized inhabitants (the "illegals") in Khao I Dang, whether registered or in hiding, presently estimated to number approximately 4,500 Cambodians. They are scheduled to be the first group moved back to the border camp. The Lawyers Committee believes that these individuals should all be immediately "legalized" and afforded universal access to food, medical attention and UNHCR protection, as well as access to resettlement abroad.

11. Legal protection should be provided to asylum seekers in Thailand on a non-discriminatory basis. The Lawyers Committee thus recommends that the UNHCR protection mandate be extended to Cambodians along the Thai-Cambodian border.

12. Asylum seekers should not be forced against their will to remain in any camp under any political faction. The Lawyers Committee recommends that a mechanism be established to facilitate the prompt transfer of a camp resident to another camp for appropriate reasons, including family reunification, or protection of an individual who is threatened or placed in danger.

III.   PRINCIPAL   PROCESSING   CONCLUSIONS   AND RECOMMENDATIONS

1. The Immigration and Naturalization Service (INS) refugee processing system is conducted and viewed largely as an extra-legal process. Applicants are not represented by counsel or an advocate, are not informed of the basis for a decision denying them refugee status and have only limited rights of appeal based on the introduction of new evidence.   There is no transcript of INS processing interviews and INS files are regarded as confidential and accessible only to U.S. government officials.

The Lawyers Committee recommends that INS processing be afforded the safeguards, protections and procedures common to U.S. administrative and judicial processes. Applicants for refugee status should have access to meaningful counsel and advocates should be permitted to accompany the applicant into an interview and participate therein if necessary. INS interviews, with the consent of the applicant, should be taped so that there is a record of these proceedings.   The Lawyers Committee also recommends that applicants' right to appeal be expanded and not be restricted solely to cases involving new evidence or legal developments. Such measures would introduce a degree of fairness presently absent from the refugee processing system.

2. The U.S. refugee processing system is subject to extreme resource restrictions, including the limited number of INS staff officers assigned in Bangkok. There should be sufficient officers to conduct adequate and thorough adjudication of the numerous pending cases. To accommodate the chronic shortage of INS officers and large number of pending cases, INS has in the past employed on a temporary basis Temporary Duty (TDY) officers to process applicants for refugee status. The use of TDY officers exacerbates existing problems because these individuals lack critical background and experience in applicable legal standards and in country conditions necessary to make an informed and considered decision as to refugee status. Indeed, past experience has shown that determinations by TDY officers may not be as accurate and reliable as determinations by permanent officers. Accordingly, the Lawyers Committee urges that the use of TDY officers should be ended and only permanent duty officers should conduct refugee status interviews.

3. The INS officers involved in processing -- including the permanent officers -- generally have no background in Southeast Asian affairs. Affirmative recruitment of persons experienced in

10

Cambodian, Laotian, or Vietnamese affairs should be undertaken. This applies to INS interviewers and adjudicators, as well as to Ethnic Affairs Officers and Joint Voluntary Agency caseworkers who are involved in other preliminary processing and assessment of refugee status.

4. There is little doubt that the processing of Cambodians, Vietnamese and Laotians is a delicate and difficult task requiring a great deal of background and training. Nonetheless, in the past, INS officers have received no training prior to undertaking reviews. While the Lawyers Committee in January 1988 was informed that a training program would be established sometime in the future, as of October 1988, nine months later, a formal training program had not been established. The Lawyers Committee urges the establishment of a formal training program for new officers, including training on applicable legal standards and guidelines, as well as on language and culture. Such training should include input from non-governmental organizations and the UNHCR.

5. The Lawyers Committee also suggests that continuing educational programs should be created in order to provide updates on legal issues, current country conditions, and issues which arise during the adjudication process. In addition, a current library of materials on conditions in Cambodia, Laos, and Vietnam should be available to INS officers, in order to supplement information available in the country conditions reports. Training and practice materials should also be developed to help INS officers learn to effectively use translators, a problem which continues to plague the interviewing process.

6. The lack of consistency and reliability in the processing system is highlighted by the varying rates of approvals and rejections among the various interviewers. While in January 1988 the Lawyers Committee was informed that a tracking system was going to be established, no such system has been formally established. Instead, one INS officer has instituted an informal monitoring system on a weekly basis which looks at approval and rejection rates generally -- not for individual officers. While such a system is commendable, the Lawyers Committee supports the development of an institutionalized quality control system in order to oversee the acceptance/rejection rates of individual INS officers. Such records should be kept in order to assure that acceptance rates do not vary greatly among individuals, suggesting idiosyncratic enforcement of refugee criteria. In addition, individual cases should be reviewed and discussed on a periodic basis in order to ensure that determinations are consistent between interviewers.

11

7. The Worldwide Guidelines for Overseas Refugee Processing (Guidelines) currently utilized by INS were published in 1983. Since 1983, there have been many changes which have rendered these guidelines obsolete, such as the Supreme Court's decision in Cardoza-Fonseca, setting forth the appropriate standard of proof by which adjudicators are to assess refugee claims. The 1983 Guidelines are also inadequate since they are often vague and contain minimal guidance for assessing whether an applicant qualifies as a refugee. The Guidelines are particularly deficient in three critical areas which provide the basis for many rejections -- whether a person has participated in the persecution of others, is not believable, or faces economic persecution.

The Lawyers Committee recommends that the Guidelines be updated and revised to reflect current legal and factual information and to provide clear and detailed guidance to staff officers. In particular, the Guidelines should contain current guidance as to the Cardoza-Fonseca standard for refugee status and the applicability of that standard to previously decided cases. The Guidelines should also address in detail the manner of determining what persons are unworthy of refugee protection based upon participation in persecution, how to fairly assess and give the benefit of the doubt to refugees in assessing their credibility, and the circumstances under which "persecution" can be economic in character and yet warrant refugee protection. The Guidelines should be revised to include criteria so that denial of refugee status is based upon reliable evidence and not upon rumor, hearsay or unfounded "stereotypes" as well as to ensure the "persecutor" exception is not subject to impermissibly broad interpretation by individual interviewing officers.

8. INS refugee adjudicators rely on country condition reports on Cambodia, Laos and Vietnam dating from 1983 -- reports which have been widely characterized as outdated and deficient. These reports provide background and factual information often necessary to make a determination as to refugee status and are one of the few source materials available to INS officers. Such inaccurate reports have a direct impact; a number of rejected cases examined by the Lawyers Committee suggest that they have been improperly rejected by INS based on a combination of improper criteria and generalizations about country conditions that are unfounded in fact. The most common problem is the use of generalized "stereotypes" about country conditions, such as unfounded beliefs that Cambodians engaged in certain activities and from certain areas supported the Khmer Rouge. Such cases point to the need for reliable country

condition information in order to accurately evaluate an individual's claim to refugee status.

Accordingly, the Lawyers Committee suggests that country condition reports should be updated to the present and should be revised on at least an annual basis. While some updated information has been provided piecemeal, a unified series of country reports, incorporating current available knowledge, is clearly necessary.

9. Under confidentiality guidelines recently promulgated, INS adjudicators cannot inform a rejected applicant of the reasons for the denial of refugee status. This persistent lack of available information has mystified an already nebulous process.

The Lawyers Committee urges that the guidelines be revised to inform applicants the basis for a decision denying refugee status. In this manner, review of reasons for denial will be facilitated, possible errors in decisions can be spotted more expeditiously and quality control can be more effectively managed. While INS officers are currently permitted to inform a rejected applicant which additional documents may be necessary to support a claim, such information may not be helpful given the fact that refugees are frequently without documentation to confirm their claims for protection.

10. At the present time, INS adjudicators place an inordinate emphasis on documentation. Such emphasis, however, ignores cultural and factual realities since many individuals may have destroyed personal records and identifications in an attempt to hide aspects of their identity, such as military or government service, from the Khmer Rouge or Pathet Lao.

The Lawyers Committee suggests that adjudication guidelines make clear that discrepancies in family tree information and lack of documentation should not be considered dispositive in terms of denial. Such information is useful in order to determine relationships and test credibility, but ultimately INS officers must determine on a case-by-case basis whether or not an individual has a "well-founded fear of persecution." Minor discrepancies should not serve as the ground for denial of claims. Written findings and reasons should be available so that it can be determined on review whether the discrepancies or lack of documentation are minor or material.

11. There is currently no formal mechanism for administrative or judicial review of decisions denying refugee status. An appellate process should be routinely available in the Department of Justice to

enable individuals to appeal any adverse determinations to a neutral non-INS arbiter. Such a process should be based on review of written findings and reasons for rejection made by INS officers. Judicial reviews also should be available in appropriate circumstances. Allowing such review would promote fairness.

12. There are over 10,000 Cambodians at Khao I Dang who have been denied refugee status by U.S. immigration authorities. There is substantial controversy relating to these rejected cases. Many believe that valid refugee claims have been improperly rejected by the INS based on improper findings of participation in Khmer Rouge persecution. Additionally, upon the anticipated closing of Khao I Dang, these individuals face the prospect of being forcibly moved to a border camp, the loss of their neutrality and the compromise of their protection under the mandate of UNHCR as a result of such a move.

The Lawyers Committee suggests that the rejected cases at Khao I Dang should be re-reviewed, even by a special Justice Department panel, utilizing revised "persecution" guidelines and updated country condition information. Such a review should not be undertaken by individuals who had a substantive role in the prior determinations. Applicants should be personally re-interviewed and afforded an opportunity to submit supplemental information.

13. The U.S. humanitarian parole program should be expanded to respond to the protection problems experienced by asylum seekers in Thailand and made available to them on a non-discriminatory basis. Individuals with compelling cases for parole into the United States might include women and children who have been victimized by rape or other similar abuse.

IV. PROTECTION ISSUES ON THE THAI-CAMBODIAN BORDER: Cambodians and Land Vietnamese

There are nine known[6] bamboo-and-thatch communities for asylum seekers along Thailand's volatile 400-mile frontier with the People's Republic of Kampuchea (PRK). These camps hold approximately 330,000 survivors of the post-1975 murderous Khmer Rouge rule in Cambodia, as well as Vietnamese land and boat people. All but two of these camps, Khao I Dang and the Ban Thad section of Site 2, are overseen by the UNBRO with the support of the ICRC and international voluntary agencies and a variety of Thai organizations.

Each camp is administered by political components of the Coalition Government of Democratic Kampuchea (CGDK), the tripartite Cambodian resistance coalition whose guerrillas have been waging a ten-year war against the Vietnamese occupation of their homeland. In response, the Vietnamese army (PAVN) and surrogate PRK forces have often targeted the camps' civilian populations. Between 1982 and the 1984-85 "dry season" offensive, when all Cambodian refugees were forced onto Thai territory, UNBRO and ICRC evacuated border camps on 85 occasions. Many of the evacuations were performed while artillery shells were falling.

In 1988, although direct shelling of Site 2 has been sporadic, camps under Khmer Rouge control have been shelled and in some cases civilians have been killed. During one month -- July 1988 -- the following incidents of shelling and casualties were reported:

---

[6] Along the border there are also a series of hidden "satellite" camps, primarily under the control of the Khmer Rouge. The civilian population of these camps is substantial, though largely unknown.

-- On July 1, 1988, there was shelling in the area of Nong Sang and Nong Samet.

-- During the week of July 4-8, 1988, fighting was reported approximately 20 kilometers from Site 2, in the area of O'Bok, and in Phnom Malai near Aranyaprathet.

-- On July 12, 1988, Site 8 was shelled between 7:10 and 7:26 a.m. According to Thai and Khmer sources, 8 shells fell on the camp, killing 4 people and wounding an additional 12 people. Panic was reported in the population; approximately 100 people ran behind the camp towards the mountains, where they remained for two days. Since then, individuals have dug bunkers near their homes.

-- On July 18, 1988, Bo Rai was shelled at approximately 8:30 a.m. Three shells fell on the camp and one shell fell outside the camp. One person was reportedly injured and was evacuated to a Khmer Rouge hospital. The UNBRO school building was destroyed.

-- On July 25, 1988, there was shelling in the area of Khlong Nam Sai. Three hundred Thai villagers were evacuated from the border area. Audible shelling was heard throughout the entire week in the southern area of Trat.

The border, thus, is a virtual war zone under martial control of the Thai military. Access to the camps is restricted to local Thai or foreign visitors, except for registered relief workers, military personnel and black marketeers. After nearly 20 years of war and displacement, the Cambodians along the border remain trapped between hostile forces, denied basic human rights and unable to return home or join relatives abroad.

Many of the concerns about the protection of Cambodians set forth in the Lawyers Committee's 1987 report, Seeking Shelter, remain and new concerns have arisen. But during the January and September-October 1988 fact-finding missions to Thailand, the Lawyers Committee found that in the twelve months since the publication of our 1987 report, Thai officials responsible for Cambodian border security had initiated a number of important reforms, most notably the formation of a specifically-trained security unit, the DPPU.

During mid-1987, the Supreme Command of the Thai military, directed by General Chaovalit Yongchaiyudh, reorganized the administration for border security. An internal investigation was conducted, which resulted in the dismissal or transfer of army and paramilitary personnel involved in black market and human rights violations. A new management system was created, under the direction of Sp. Col. Sanan Kajornklam, to improve coordination with international organizations working in the camps.

As a result of studies on camp security made in cooperation with UNBRO, in April 1988, the Supreme Command announced the formation of the DPPU. In August 1988, the DPPU replaced the abusive Task Force 80 rangers as external security guards at all UN-monitored camps for Cambodians. Based on the information available to date, it would appear that the DPPU is a marked improvement over their predecessors and have performed their duties admirably.[7] Other reforms, such as implementing a legal market at Site 2 and improving primary education in the camps, are encouraging.

Despite these positive developments, the Committee also received reports of rising incidents of violence perpetrated by Cambodians against other Cambodians -- incidents which are largely unaddressed and unpunished due to the complete absence of rule of law. A range of factors provide the backdrop, from overcrowded and restrictive camp environments to black marketeering and banditry on both sides of the border. The easy availability of weapons and growing presence of demoralized armed guerrillas in the camps have contributed to the seemingly explosive situation. The situation is particularly grim in Site 2, where 175,000 people are tightly packed in an area of approximately 7.5 square kilometers and easily within shelling range.

---

[7] On October 6, 1988, during a meeting with the directors of various international voluntary agencies in Bangkok, the Lawyers Committee delegation of Arthur Helton, Roni Rubenstein and Al Santoli was told that the DPPU have been largely "professional and humane" in the camps and the DPPU leadership was "very receptive to suggestions" presented by the international community.

A. Background: The Cambodian Exodus

1. The Flight

After seizing power in April 1975, the Khmer Rouge emptied Cambodia's urban centers and instituted slave-labor communes. A ruthless campaign to reshape the fabric of Khmer society led to the decimation of most educated, religious and free-enterprise oriented Cambodians. All told, between a million to three million people -- up to a third of the population -- perished from starvation, disease, the punishing rigors of forced labor, and outright execution.[8]

In December 1978, the PAVN invaded Cambodia. After capturing the capital, Phnom Penh, in January 1979, a surrogate regime was installed, headed by Heng Samrin and Hun Sen, former Khmer Rouge officers.

During the first months of the invasion, thousands of destitute Cambodian survivors, fearing another repressive regime, began an exodus toward the Thai border. The less fortunate were herded at gunpoint by retreating Khmer Rouge into malaria-infested forests in the Cardamom mountains.[9] By mid-1979, with the country on the edge of famine, the PAVN siphoned off the small amount of international relief permitted into the country. A deluge of rag-clad, starving asylum seekers massed in open fields along the Thai frontier.

Thai officials, fearing an overwhelming influx, responded violently. In June 1979, some 40,000 Cambodian men, women and children were bused to Preah Vihear, a remote area, and forced at gunpoint down a steep mountain into a minefield. Thousands were killed or maimed. Nonetheless, thousands of Cambodian asylum seekers continued to arrive at the border, including famished "walking skeletons" herded by brutal Khmer Rouge fighters.

---

[8] See Haing Ngor, *A Cambodian Odyssey* (1988); Elizabeth Becker, *When the War Was Over* (1987).

[9] See Timothy Carney, *Kampuchea: Balance of Survival* (1983); William Shawcross, *The Quality of Mercy* (1984); Al Santoli, *To Bear Any Burden* (1985).

In response to international outcry, in October 1979 the Royal Thai Government created "holding centers" for Cambodians pending resettlement in third countries. Fearing Vietnamese military encroachment, the Thai permitted the People's Republic of China to resupply the Khmer Rouge for guerrilla activities.[10]

Non-communist movements also formed along the border. Former soldiers of the pre-1975 Khmer Republic, who had previously fought in small bands against the Khmer Rouge, competed with Khmer warlords who dominated lucrative border smuggling operations. In October 1979, several of these groups united to form the Khmer People's National Liberation Front (KPNLF) under the political leadership of 70-year-old former Prime Minister, Son Sann. Other groups loyal to former monarch Norodom Sihanouk united in 1981 to form the Sihanoukist National Army (ANS), the military arm of the royalist United Front for an Independent, Neutral Peaceful and Cooperative Cambodia (FUNCINPEC).

In 1982, the disparate resistance factions formed an uneasy coalition government, the CGDK, in order to win diplomatic support at the UN and material support from the People's Republic of China, ASEAN and the West. With varying degrees of cooperation or force, individuals on the border were placed under control of the resistance factions.

2. Establishment of the Border Camps

Forceful Thai actions, such as the Preah Vihear "push-back," provoked international commitments to share the burden of displaced Cambodians. Cyrus Vance, the U.S. Secretary of State, promised generous resettlement. Other Western nations and the UNHCR offered similar assurances. As a result, Thailand adopted a more generous policy toward the Cambodians fleeing for safety to frontier enclaves.

In September 1979, the ICRC, UNBRO and the United Nations International Childrens' Educational Fund (UNICEF) created

---

[10] See Lawyers Committee for Human Rights, *Kampuchea: After the Worst* (1985); William Shawcross, *The Quality of Mercy* (1984).

a joint medical and feeding operation on the border.[11]   The Thai
government announced that "Khmer aliens" could enter UNHCR-
administered camps. Khao I Dang, the largest of these camps, located
less than eight miles from the border, was created for refugees not
under Khmer Rouge control. By early 1980, Khao I Dang housed
150,000 refugees. Smaller camps outside Khmer Rouge control, often
uprooted by border violence and dominated by rival warlords, were
supplied by approximately 95 humanitarian agencies.   Thirty-four
thousand Khmer Rouge soldiers and civilians under their control were
moved to an inland site known as Sakeo Holding Center.[12]

By the end of 1979, a shifting displaced population, estimated
by Thai authorities at more than one million, congregated around
border aid centers. The Thai worried that the large population would
overwhelm resettlement programs and act as a magnet to attract more
Cambodians. Consequently, in January 1980, Khao I Dang and other
holding centers were officially closed to new arrivals. A new Thai
security force, Task Force 80, comprised of poorly trained local
recruits called "rangers," was created to provide security around the
border camps.

Thai policy classified Cambodian asylum seekers residing in
the border camps as "illegal aliens" or "displaced persons." Thus, they
were denied the legal protection afforded to refugees and the chance
to be accepted for resettlement by a third country.   Thailand's
restrictive policy was fed by concern that Thai border villages were
endangered by the Cambodian presence.   Ethnic hostilities and
economic dislocation of its citizens threatened to engender domestic
political tensions.[13]

---

[11] In 1982, with the Khmer-displaced population estimated at
250,000, UNBRO was created to coordinate services provided to
Cambodians in border camps.

[12] See Timothy Carney, *Kampuchea: A Balance of Survival*
(1983).

[13] Programs related to the international relief effort have
attempted to address some of these concerns. UNBRO assistance,
including water, education and nutrition, has been directed to some
170 affected Thai border villages. Local economies have also been
boosted by the local business patronage of voluntary agency personnel

During the winter and spring of 1984-85, the Vietnamese army launched a devastating dry-season offensive that destroyed most camps and border resistance bases. Nearly 250,000 Cambodians fled into Thailand and were sheltered in UNBRO evacuation sites located a few miles within Thai territory.

Unlike the aftermath of previous offensives, Vietnamese and PRK forces occupied the destroyed border camps. To seal the border area, Cambodian citizens throughout the country were conscripted into forced labor brigades to dig booby-trapped trenches, lay minefields and construct bamboo fences.

In early 1985, with hostile forces preventing asylum seekers from returning to Cambodian territory, the Thai government agreed to an UNBRO proposal to build eight temporary camps inside of Thailand, though still within range of artillery fire. Almost overnight, UNBRO-provided blue-plastic and bamboo hut communities were constructed along the border.

Each of the border camps is administered by personnel closely identified with one of the guerrilla groups forming the Coalition opposing the Vietnam-backed government in Phnom Penh. Cambodian civilian administrators supervise the daily administration of the camps.

As of September 1988, there were more than 315,000 Cambodians and Vietnamese residing in camps along Thailand's borders. (This figure, however, excludes Cambodians held along the "hidden border," as well as those who have been forcibly moved by the Khmer Rouge.) The KPNLF administers the majority of the border population. Site 2, which is approximately one mile from the border, houses the largest concentration of displaced Cambodians. As of September 1988, there were approximately 170,000 Khmer in Site 2. In addition, Site 2 housed roughly 3,500 Vietnamese in the Ban Thad section, 1,800 in the area known as the Platform and 2,000 in

---

living in towns near the border and remittances from overseas relatives received by Cambodian camp residents. However, the Thai government feared and still continues to fear that impoverished Thai villagers along the border will be angered by the spectre of permanent or thriving Khmer communities.

Section 5.[14] Sok Sann, located in southern Trat Province, housed roughly 8,000 Cambodians.

As of September 1988, Site B, which is in the mountainous Surin Province, housed approximately 55,000 Sihanouk Loyalists. It is FUNCINPEC's only settlement.

The Khmer Rouge retain tight control over approximately 60,000 civilians in four or five camps, interspersed along the northern, central and southern border regions. As of September 1988, the largest camp, Site 8, housed approximately 34,000 Cambodians. Other Khmer Rouge camps include O'Trao with approximately 16,500 Cambodians, Bo Rai with 4,000 Cambodians and Ta Luan with 2,000 Cambodians. In addition, as of June 1988, there were reportedly roughly 2,800 Cambodians in O'Panko and 1,500 in Sanrong Kiat. These people, however, were moved from these camps. Although their whereabouts were unknown as of September 1988, subsequent reports indicated that about 6,000 people are squatting in makeshift camps near Ta Luan.

Finally, as of September 1988, there were approximately 14,500 Cambodians in Khao I Dang, which is administered by the Thai government in cooperation with UNHCR. This figure, however, excludes the substantial illegal population in the camp, which is estimated at approximately 3,000 Cambodians.

B.   Thai Policy: "Humane Deterrence"

In order to discourage the border Cambodians from considering the camps as permanent settlements, Thai authorities have precluded resettlement or integration in the local community and enforced austere conditions. Only the bare necessities for survival are provided and Thai security officers, under Task Force 80 command, often resorted to ruthless methods and inhumane treatment with no meaningful prospect of discipline or punishment. A policy of deliberate indifference to deprived circumstances and abuse is incompatible with human rights standards.

---

[14]   Following the completion of resettlement interviews of Platform and Section 5 residents by embassies of resettling countries in November 1988, some 2,800 rejected "land Vietnamese" were prepared to be consolidated into the Ban Thad section with Vietnamese "boat people."

A major factor contributing to the Thai government's restrictive policy toward Cambodians is fear that, as international interest wanes, Thailand will be left to shoulder -- at its own expense -- a substantial refugee population of asylum seekers.[15] Thai officials and opinion makers continue to emphasize that "refugees must not remain in this country indefinitely."[16]

Mr. Sawat Daranond, an official at the Thai National Security Council, told the Lawyers Committee in January 1988 that the large border camp population has also created a "negative impact" on local Thai communities in terms of land allocation, deforestation and security problems. Kobsak Chutikul, Director of the Foreign Ministry's Social Division, told the Lawyers Committee delegation in January 1988 "that [public] perception of a permanent refugee problem for Thailand will create [domestic] hostility." According to Kobsak, certain quarters say, "Where is it going to stop? They will be moving into Bangkok one day."

Thailand's policy towards the Cambodians living along its border is integrally connected to Thailand's security needs and geo-political interests. A substantial Khmer border population serves as a reluctant human buffer against Vietnamese military encroachment

---

[15] Since the early 1950's Thailand has borne the residual consequences of ongoing wars in neighboring countries. During the early 1950's Thailand granted temporary asylum to some 70,000 "Dienbienphu" North Vietnamese refugees. Today, most of that population and their descendants remain largely unassimilated in Thailand's northeastern provinces. Thai officials have often referred to the "bitter experience" of harboring this population. The generosity, however ambivalent, shown by the Thai government and people toward more than a million of their neighbors in need of protection deserves both respect and encouragement. The armed conflicts that threaten to spill over Thailand's borders with Laos, Cambodia and Malaysia, as well as Burma, have strained the kingdom's defense manpower and resources.

[16] See "Conference Discusses Plight of Refugees," The Nation (Bangkok) June 6, 1987, at 5.

and provides the resistance coalition with political legitimacy.[17] At the same time, however, Thailand has sought to prevent this population from growing to unmanageable proportions or developing a permanent economic or political structure that could threaten Thai sovereignty.

To dissuade Cambodian asylum seekers from considering permanent relocation, Thai officials in a compromise with Western officials enforced deterrent conditions in the camps. Especially in Site 2, this has resulted in crowded living quarters, physical confinement, limited education programs and the denial of a means to earn a living. International health professionals in the camps have told the Lawyers Committee that the stress imposed on camp residents by the austere "deterrent" conditions have led to a potentially explosive situation.[18]

C. Site 2: 170,000 at Risk

With a population of more than 170,000 Cambodians and 6,000 Vietnamese, Site 2 is the second largest Cambodian city in the world and the third largest community in Thailand. Despite this substantial population, Site 2 does not have a rule of law. Criminals, who are rarely apprehended or punished, generally are not held responsible for abuses.

---

[17] Dr. Prachyada Tavedikul, a former Thai government official, remarked at the 1987 CCSDPT Conference in Thailand: "[The refugees] serve a practical, political purpose. They provide international recognition and . . . are also a buffer for Thailand against its potential adversaries. The anti-Vietnamese Coalition Government of Democratic Kampuchea needs the civilians in the frontier region to ensure its legitimacy."

[18] Most members of voluntary agencies interviewed by the Lawyers Committee requested anonymity since they feared expulsion or other forms of retaliation. Such concerns appear justified. For example, in May 1988, following a written appeal to the U.S. government by seven voluntary agencies concerning Thailand's policy to deny safe haven to Vietnamese boat people, a spokesman for the Thai Ministry of the Interior threatened to "take appropriate action" against the agencies involved.

In January and October 1988, the Lawyers Committee delegation twice visited Site 2, toured the entire camp and spoke with directors of or volunteers from most international organizations that provide services in the camp. During the January visit, Thai security officials restricted the delegation's interviews of camp residents and Task Force 80 personnel were present at all times. Their attitude reinforced claims by relief workers of intimidation by Thai security officers and made it difficult to monitor and report human rights abuses in the camp.

During the October visit, the Lawyers Committee found the newly-assigned DPPU, who permitted unrestricted interviews, to be accommodating. Important reforms were evident in improved security and expanded camp facilities. However, a number of serious human rights concerns in the camp persist.

During the first half of 1988, an alarming rise in domestic violence and suicide attempts was reported in Site 2. A consortium of international relief workers expressed urgent concern about "rapidly deteriorating" social conditions among the camp's 170,000 inhabitants. These include overcrowding, shortages of water and cooking fuel, the stress of being confined within range of hostile forces, fear of repatriation, as well as harassment by Task Force 80 security guards known for violent abuses.

The presence of hundreds of disenfranchised guerrillas and the readily available supply of weapons has caused security experts to warn of a potential armed conflict within the camp. KPNLF administrators responsible for internal camp security have been repeatedly criticized for violent and illicit behavior. Forest-based armed brigands often linked to black market smuggling activities have terrorized camp residents. Nearby Thai villages have been similarly victimized by Khmer gangs carrying automatic weapons and rocket-propelled grenades. Kidnapping rings that reach into Cambodian communities in the U.S. have demanded ransoms for abducted family members. Despite these considerable abuses, there is no enforceable legal system in the camp to protect victims or punish perpetrators of crimes.

1. Lawlessness Among Camp Inhabitants

Medical reports from camp medical facilities and statistical graphs compiled by medical workers in April 1988 document a steep rise in violence and suicide attempts seen at camp hospitals. In a meeting with the Lawyers Committee on May 12, 1988, a doctor, who had just returned from working at Site 2 and KID, emphasized:

25

Camp residents are growing more desperate. We had more than 10 suicide attempts a month reported in Site Two South alone, including people leaping into steep ditches or hanging themselves. . . . We've seen increasing numbers of child abuse cases. Children under 10 years old have come in with venereal diseases. That's indicative of how social mores and hope in the camp are breaking down. People are losing control.

In a June 13, 1988 written statement submitted to various international and voluntary agencies, including UNHCR, UNBRO and the U.S. Embassy, a group of relief workers from several agencies in Site 2 stated:

The number of reported cases of violence/harassment in Site 2 has increased 100 percent since last year. Suicide attempts have risen sharply, as well as admission to the hospital due to violence and trauma. Incidents such as arguments over water or quarrels between children have escalated into beatings and murder by bamboo sticks and axes.

Between January and May 1988, UNBRO statistics indicate that 357 individuals were treated in camp hospitals due to violent incidents. These cases showed a serious escalating trend: in January, 67 cases were treated; February, 83 cases; March, 99 cases and May, 108 cases. In contrast, 455 cases were reported for all of 1987. Of the cases reported from January to May 1988, 55 percent of the cases were beatings; 54 percent were outside-of-family incidents. Medical workers in Site 2 told the Lawyers Committee that these reported cases do not nearly represent the scope of the problem. Based on discussions with camp residents, they estimate that hundreds of other victims do not report for treatment out of fear or shame.

An incident in Site 2 South on April 1, 1988 is an example of the growing levels of violence among camp residents. The incident was triggered by a fight between two small children, approximately three years old. The parents joined in the dispute which soon escalated into a battle of knives and axes. One father, who had been stabbed and later died of his wounds, axed the other man's wife and children in their sleep. A two-and-a-half year old axe victim, when taken to the hospital, had to be transferred to a jail -- the only place available to protect the child from the dead man's family.

26

Reports of incidents of domestic abuse have also increased. For example, during the last week in March 1988 in the Nong Chan section of Site 2, a man killed his wife by disemboweling her with a knife in the middle of the road.

Such incidents of domestic abuse are rarely investigated and perpetrators are rarely punished. Relief workers in Site 2, during the Committee's October 1988 visit, emphasized the lack of protection for women abused by their husbands. According to one relief worker, "these women have little recourse but to hide in other sections of the camp. However, when the husband finds her and drags her home, there is no legal protection or shelter. The 20- to 40-year-old age group are most vulnerable." Hospital records establish that the highest rate of suicide attempts in camp is consistently among this group. The hospital recorded 37 suicide attempts in Site 2 South between July and September 1988. These included 2 men and 35 women in their twenties and thirties.

Rapes and incidents of sexual abuse have also been reported. One ICRC official in June 1987 stated that rapes in Site 2 are a common occurrence. A doctor in the camp told the Committee that communicable venereal diseases treated at the hospital, such as gonorrhea, were found in children as young as seven and eight years old. Relief officials, who have observed an increase in cases of violence and sexual abuse during periods when large numbers of KPNLF guerrillas are present in the camp, express concern that known perpetrators of violence against women or children, especially in Site 2 South, are consistently released after only "a few days" of confinement by the camp administration.[19] To encourage abused

---

[19] In a written statement of concern dated June 13, 1988, relief workers in Site 2 emphasized:

Support for the existing systems of justice must be strengthened . . . international protection officers with night access to the sites is necessary. Arbitrary enforcement of rules and laws by security and military forces must end. Individuals committing crimes against displaced persons must be brought to justice regardless of their nationality. This must be accompanied by increased accountability of those funding and supporting the border programs and protection systems.

women to come forward, ICRC has assigned a female field officer to Site 2.

Khmer camp leaders told the Lawyers Committee that incidents of violence among camp residents are caused by a variety of factors, ranging from "boredom and depression," to overcrowding and the "lack of meaningful activities," especially during dry season water shortages.[20] In addition, a number of violent disputes have reportedly erupted over water, which at times has been in short supply.

The Thai government has continually rejected requests by UNBRO and other voluntary agencies to remain in the Khmer camp at night when most violent abuses occur. Thai officials claim that such a presence "would be more symbolic than practical in security terms."[21]

The Thai government maintains that KPNLF's status is that of a "government in exile," and therefore the KPNLF must assume primary responsibility for maintaining law and order in Site 2. But this assertion by the Thai authorities is contrary to basic principles of international law respecting state sovereignty and jurisdiction.[22]

Resolution of incidents among Cambodians is left to internal camp administration. But in October 1988 discussions with Thai Supreme Command and KPNLF officials, however, the Committee found that Khmer leaders displayed a disturbing lack of enthusiasm

---

[20] Interview of Thou Thon, Khmer administrator of Rithisen, and Chhay Kim Hour, administrator of Nong Chan, by Al Santoli, Site 2, October 4, 1988.

[21] Written statement by Royal Thai Government, "On the Concerns of Senator Hatfield and Others Over Security at Site 2," December 4, 1987.

[22] See A. Helton, "Asylum and Refugee Protection in Thailand," 1 International Journal of Refugee Law (1989) (forthcoming).

for enforcing a unified legal code within the camp.[23] Moreover, for more than three years the Front has been torn by factional rivalries, which have made the organization ungovernable. The camp has been under the High Command of the KPNLF military, headed by Gen. Sak Sutsakhan, whose dissident faction has waged a two-year campaign to seize control of the KPNLF from Son Sann. Control of the camp's population is a central aspect of the power struggle.

The Front's political leader, Son Sann, has conveyed to the Lawyers Committee a willingness to address reports of human rights violations committed in KPNLF's areas of control. Yet, due to the bitter split within the Front, until May 1988, the Thai government repeatedly denied Son Sann permission to visit the border area. In addition, KPNLF leaders loyal to Son Sann, such as Chea Chhut and his deputies, are known to have systematically abused asylum seekers.

On May 27, 1988, a spokesman for Son Sann announced that the civilian leadership of the KPNLF wished to form a "central administrative committee" to replace military control of Site 2. The proposed administrative committee's members were reportedly nominated by Section administrators in Site 2.

In the past, however, Son Sann and rival civilian leadership have been reluctant to investigate alleged abuses by officials. For example, on May 8, 1988, armed KPNLF soldiers entered the COERR hospital in Site 2 North, accompanied by a deputy security official of Nong Chan section. They demanded to see a young midwife, Miss Sany (alias), 20, and said their commander, Ben Pirun, was outside looking for her. According to witnesses, the girl went into hiding while the 10-15 armed KPNLF soldiers searched the hospital for her. Protected by camp residents, Miss Sany was eventually transferred by international agencies to another camp with her mother for her protection.

Western observers in Bangkok told the Lawyers Committee that upon receiving reports of the incident from relief officials, Son Sann defended Pirun, who is reportedly a protege of banned warlord

---

[23] Interview of Sp. Col. Somsak Srisupundit, Command Center for Relief of Kampucheans by Arthur Helton and Al Santoli, Bangkok, October 7, 1988; Interview of Col. Hath Wirasamrith, DPPU Commander and Cambodian camp leaders by Al Santoli, Site 2, October 3, 1988.

Sann defended Pirun, who is reportedly a protege of banned warlord Chea Chhut. In a meeting with the Lawyers Committee on October 19, 1988 in New York, although Son Sann invited the Committee and Amnesty International to investigate his organization, he sought to defend the actions of Pirun.[24]

2. The Proliferation of Weapons

The growing availability of weapons in Site 2 has contributed to the escalating levels of violence reported in the camp. Small arms, such as hand grenades, can be readily purchased in the camp and on the black market. A former medical volunteer in Site 2 told the Lawyers Committee that she was able to purchase fourteen grenades for four dollars in the Nong Chan section's black market.

According to camp leaders and relief workers, hand grenades have become the "preferred weapon" within the camp. To circumvent DPPU efforts to restrict weapons in the camp, some KPNLF soldiers and deserters bury their rifles just outside the camp perimeter and carry hand grenades, which are easier to conceal.

In April 1988, in the Ampil section of Site 2 North, Khmer administrators collected 90 grenades, 20 AK-47 rifles and 1,000 bullets during a one-day "reward for ammunition" scheme. Following a similar weapons collection during September 1988 in Ampil, camp leaders turned over 40 grenades and 20 rifles to the DPPU. Although only Ampil has pursued this program since early 1988, the DPPU is now encouraging the other sections to participate in similar efforts on a routine basis.

The availability of grenades in Site 2 is demonstrated by the numerous incidents involving grenades reported in the camp. During August and September 1988, UNBRO recorded approximately 20 grenade incidents in and around the camp. On March 18, 1988, two people were arrested following a grenade incident in which one person was wounded and on June 10, 1988, a small child was killed by a grenade.

---

[24] Interview of Son Sann by Al Santoli, New York, October 19, 1988. At this meeting Son Sann requested that the Lawyers Committee recommend that Chea Chhut and Liv Ne, both banned from the border for repeated human rights abuses, be returned to the border "to help me create order in the camp."

Incidents involving guns have also been reported. For example, on January 13, 1988, a woman was treated in Nong Chan hospital in Site 2 North for a bullet hole in her leg. Reportedly, she had been hit in broad daylight by a random shot fired into the camp by an unknown Khmer or Thai assailant.

3. Presence of KPNLF Soldiers in the Camp

On November 15, 1987, Svay Chek, a KPNLF officer, slipped a hand grenade into a Site 2 hut where his ex-wife was having dinner with friends. It exploded and killed a four-year-old boy and wounded seven other persons. Following the incident, civilian administrators' attempts to arrest Chek were obstructed by his military superiors. In January 1988, Chek was finally apprehended as a result of UNBRO pressure. His sentence of one year in camp jail drew further protests from international agencies. At retrial in March 1988, he was given a seven-year term at Dang Rek section jail in Site 2. Svay Chek, however, escaped in mid-September 1988. Relief officials say little effort has been made by KPNLF officials to find him.

The Svay Chek case typifies serious protection problems posed by large numbers of KPNLF soldiers or deserters in Site 2. Their presence continues to be a major cause of violence and lawlessness within the civilian camp. Some relief officials estimate that up to 4,000 armed KPNLF combatants may be inside Site 2 at any given time. A bitter feud among the Front's leadership has paralyzed military operations inside Cambodia. As a result, demoralized troops have deserted or entered Site 2 on "extended leave."

Camp violence involving KPNLF soldiers and deserters appears to be inspired by a variety of causes. Incidents of violence have erupted over gambling operations, the sale of alcohol, adultery and prostitution.[25]

In the past, when UNBRO and the ICRC have complained to KPNLF leaders about violent abuses, robberies or other incidents, either nothing was done to punish offenders or summary executions

---

[25] Prostitution in the camp has increasingly become a means of survival for some women without remittances from family abroad. Widows reportedly sell for $2 and virgins for $4. See Barbara Crossette, "After the Killing Fields: Cambodia's Forgotten Refugees," New York Times Magazine, June 26, 1988.

may have been performed.[26]   Neither KPNLF political head Son Sann, nor military chief Gen.   Sak Sutsakhan, who also heads the feuding factions of the Front, has been able to control abuses by their forces.

In January 1987, in response to the international outcry against rampant human rights abuses by its forces, the KPNLF High Command created "A Committee of Intervention of Human Rights Violations." However, within weeks, nine guerrilla commanders -- including Chea Chhut and Liv Ne, who are the most highly criticized by human rights organizations -- were promoted to the rank of general in what KPNLF resistance sources described as a "new attempt to heal the rift in the organization."[27] Finally, in March 1988, unresolved human rights abuses by the Front caused the U.S. government to threaten to halt all aid to the KPNLF unless Chea Chhut and Liv Ne were removed from the border.

While Chhut and Ne were moved from the border in early 1988 and are restricted to a KPNLF residence in Bangkok, certain elements within the KPNLF continue to lobby for their return. In October 1988 Son Sann indicated an interest in the return of Chhut and Ne to the border "to help me create order in the camp," or "to go inside Cambodia to organize in the villages."[28] Moreover, the legacy of Chhut and Ne continues to plague the lives of border residents since the command posts of Chhut and Ne have been filled by long-time associates who have been integral players in the abusive activities along the "hidden border."

Although Chhut and Ne have allegedly committed or been involved in numerous abuses, there is no indication that they will face

---

[26] See *Seeking Shelter*, at 50-59; *After the Worst*, at 227-36.

[27] See "Son Sann Promotes Nine Commanders," The Nation (Bangkok), February 23, 1987.

[28] In an interview on October 19, 1988 in New York, Son Sann also told Al Santoli that the decision to move Chhut, Ne, Gen. Dien Del and Hing Kunthon from the border was due to U.S. government pressure. However, Del and Kunthon, who belong to the rival faction in the KPNLF split, were permitted to return to the border by Thai authorities.

prosecution.[29] Thai officials have told the Lawyers Committee that, as a sovereign government in exile, disciplinary problems within the resistance factions are the internal affairs of CGDK.[30]

4. Banditry, Extortion and the "Hidden Border"

Banditry along the Thai-Cambodian border is hardly a new phenomenon. Following the 1978 Vietnamese invasion of Cambodia, the border frontier was rampant with Thai and Khmer bandits who pillaged refugees.[31] The Thai army congregated asylum seekers into camps controlled by Cambodian "warlords" who maintained the loyalty of brutal armed gangs through lucrative black market activities. Some of these warlords, such as Chea Chhut, who rules Nong Chan, survived clashes with the Khmer Rouge, the Thai army and rival gangs, and eventually became part of the KPNLF. The areas they controlled were characterized by robberies, beatings, rapes and assassinations of some camp leaders.[32]

After the 1984-85 destruction of the border camps, discipline in the Front further unraveled. As factional fighting among the Front's leaders intensified, large numbers of troops deserted. Some formed gangs that survived -- sometimes in collaboration with Thai gangs -- through robbing and kidnapping camp inhabitants and Thai border villagers. Site 2 and Khao I Dang became terrorized by nightly bandit raids.[33]

Satellite military bases were created for KPNLF military units along the border. These camps, which included training and medical

---

[29] See *Seeking Shelter*, at 63-64.

[30] Interview of Thai officials by Diane Orentlicher and Floyd Abrams, Bangkok, January 8, 1987.

[31] See Haing Ngor, *A Cambodian Odyssey* (1988), at Chapter 34.

[32] See *Seeking Shelter*, at 60-64; *After the Worst*, at 235-50.

[33] See *Seeking Shelter*, at 53-56.

facilities as well as lodging for some guerrillas' families, became known as the "hidden border." Bases such as Nong Chan, ruled by Chea Chhut, and Rithisen (Nong Samet) and Chamkar Ko, ruled by Liv Ne, became centers for massive smuggling, extortion and violent abuses against Cambodians and Vietnamese.[34] Relatives of asylum seekers held in captivity began receiving extortion demands from Thailand. A U.S. Embassy memorandum of August 22, 1986 documented "unmistakable signs on the part of KPNLF soldiers in the area of Nong Chan to use Land Vietnamese (and Cambodian) arrivals at the border for purposes of extortion." U.S. officials, acting on information from resettlement agencies, discovered a well-organized Thai-Cambodian extortion ring that extended from the hidden border into the U.S. U.S. protection officers also confirmed reports that female asylum seekers, including girls as young as 11 years of age, were being held in hidden border bases "for long periods of time, during which they were repeatedly sexually abused."[35]

In early 1987, Lawyers Committee representatives held discussions in Bangkok with Thai military leaders and KPNLF officials which focused on measures to address the violation of human rights on the hidden border and in Site 2.[36] Simultaneously, efforts by U.S. Congressional Representatives and other officials led to Thai efforts to reform Task Force 80 and to close down the most notorious hidden border bases.

---

[34] In September 1985, KPNLF leaders in Bangkok admitted that widespread abuses were caused by elements of the Nong Chan and Chamkar Ko forces. In January 1987, KPNLF Commander-in-Chief Sak Sutsakhan publicly acknowledged that some KPLNF troops had plundered Site 2. In the presence of Thai authorities, Sak said that he would try to impose stricter control over undisciplined troops. However, in May 1988, after the military dismissed human rights allegations against two of its officials, Gen. Dien Del and Hing Kunthon, the civilian leadership of the Front challenged the findings and legitimacy of the military investigative committee. See "Son Sann Vies For Control of Refugee Camp," The Nation (Bangkok), May 28, 1988.

[35] See August 22, 1986 Embassy memorandum.

[36] See *Seeking Shelter*, at 56-58.

KPNLF military commander Sak Sutsakhan and his civilian assistant, Dr. Gaffar Peang Meth, told the Committee that strict discipline would be imposed on KPNLF forces.[37] All soldiers would be moved out of Site 2, and except for small contingents to guard border passageways, hidden border units at Chamkar Ko, Nong Samet and Nong Chan under the leadership of Liv Ne and Chea Chhut would be moved to a central "secret sanctuary" where they could be better controlled.

Thai authorities also responded to concerns expressed by the Lawyers Committee, humanitarian organizations and U.S. government officials. The Thai Supreme Command, under orders from Commander-in-Chief Gen. Chaovalit Yongchaiyudh, demanded that KPNLF leaders transfer most of their forces from Chamkar Ko and Nong Chan to a central command area. To protect Thai villagers from bandit attacks, Maj. Gen. San Siphen, commander of the Thai army's Burapha Task Force, organized a special unit comprised of army, police and civilian officials to crack down on border gangs. The unit recorded numerous clashes with bandits during April and July. In one incident, the task force, on July 16, 1987, rescued approximately 68 kidnapped Thai villagers being held for ransom by Cambodian kidnappers.[38] As a result of the Thai crackdown, bandit raids on Site 2 and Khao I Dang have largely subsided. However, a number of bandit raids have been reported in Site 2. For example, on the night of January 28, 1988, approximately 20 to 30 bandits entered Site 2 South. Surrounding a house, they threatened residents with guns and bayonets. Khmer camp police arrived and a shootout occurred.

Bandit attacks have also been reported against relief workers. On March 31, 1988, three relief workers -- a British midwife of Youth With a Mission, her Thai driver and the driver of an UNBRO water truck -- were held at gunpoint by bandits on the road between Site 2 and Aranyaprathet. Their rescue by Thai defense volunteers involved a shootout in which one bandit and one defense volunteer

---

[37] Interview of Sak Sutsakhan and Dr. Gaffar Peang Meth by Diane Orentlicher and Floyd Abrams, Thailand, January 8, 1987.

[38] See "Khmer Bandits Release 68 Thai Border Villagers," Bangkok World, July 17, 1987; Rodney Tasker, "Khmer Bandits Trouble Thais," Far Eastern Economic Review, July 9, 1987.

were killed. On leaving the camp later that evening, all relief workers at Site 2 were required to travel to and from the camp in convoys.

The DPPU has generally been effective in responding to incidents of banditry within the camp. On September 28 and October 3, 1988, armed bandits raided Section 5 of Site 2 South, which houses the Land Vietnamese. During the first incident, due to a breakdown in communication, the DPPU "reaction team" arrived after the robbery occurred. However, on October 3, 1988, the DPPU responded immediately to a radio call for help by camp security, causing the bandits to retreat.[39]

Extortion too remains a significant problem. On November 30, 1988, some Cambodian community leaders in the U.S. told the Lawyers Committee that asylum seekers have been charged "taxes" of 400 baht (approximately $16) per person to cross into KPNLF border zones and are forced to hire KPNLF "guides" for 1000 baht (approximately $40) per person to escort them to Site 2. Individuals who are unable to pay these illegal fees are held in KPNLF hidden border camps until relatives at Site 2 or abroad can send them money.Additionally, border relief workers and observers in Bangkok have told the Lawyers Committee in October 1988 that a number of Khmer, Khmer Krom and some Vietnamese residents of Site 2 had come to them in recent months worried about raising ransom money for relatives threatened with death by Khmer or Thai "guides" or smugglers, who bring refugees to the border from Cambodia. The "safehouses" that hold abductees are believed to be in local Thai towns.

Informed western observers also report that abductees are held by KPNLF forces in two hidden border "jails", the KPNLF hospital base, which can be seen from Site 2, and a second base located between Nong Samet and Chamkar Ko.

One relief worker told of at least two or three cases where brothers or sisters of Site 2 residents were kidnapped. The camp residents were charged a ransom 20,000 baht ($800). A down payment of 5,000 baht was demanded and the rest paid in installments after the victim's release.

In October 1988, ICRC staff told the Committee that "detainees are now separated into small groups, so they don't know

---

[39] Accounts of bandit attacks based on interviews with residents of Section 5 by Al Santoli, Site 2, October 4, 1988.

who else is being held in the camps, and can't report names to the ICRC." Moreover, released victims are frequently afraid to talk because, according to a relief worker, "Site 2 is controlled by the same warlords who control the border."[40]

Cambodians who have spent considerable time on the border claim that, among other extortionists, Liv Ne and Chea Chhut's successors are carrying on the same activities as their predecessors. In March and April 1988, a number of Cambodian-Americans in California reported to a representative of Amnesty International that they had received extortion letters from Thailand. The hidden border areas of Nong Chan and Nong Samet were again identified as kidnapping centers in these letters.

Officials of the ICRC, which has the protection mandate for all asylum seekers along the Cambodian frontier, continue to express frustration about being denied access to hidden border bases. For example, on October 29, 1987, during the debriefing of 21 Vietnamese released from a KPNLF base near Site 2, ICRC officials learned that 11 more females were being held by guerrillas. It took a week of negotiations with the guerrillas before the abductees' release was finally arranged.

Beside KPNLF hidden bases and bandits camped in the mountains, another Khmer group known as "the Cobra Team," who are identified by their soldier patches, are reportedly involved in extortion and abuse of asylum seekers. The Cobras are believed to operate in the Chamkar Ko border passage area, previously dominated by banished KPNLF commander Liv Ne. It is reported that Cobras are connected to the Thai army.[41]

Other extortion rings are run by Thai-Cambodian syndicates that smuggle residents out of Site 2 to safehouses in Bangkok. The kidnappers make collect phone calls to Cambodians in the U.S., demanding ransoms of $3,000 to $10,000 and threatening physical abuse or death to the abducted family member.

---

[40] Interview of international relief organizations by Al Santoli, Site 2, October 3-5, 1988.

[41] Informed observers told the Committee that the Cobra leader, reportedly named Koeuth Sam Rouy (which may be an alias), claims to be a translator for Thai Task Force 838.

37

A recent case illustrates the problem. On April 4, 1987, Mrs. Sok Phoeuth, 22, and her four-year-old daughter were driven out of Site 2 in broad daylight by armed Thai men in military officers' uniforms. A Cambodian contact man in the camp's black market had promised that they could help her to join her parents in America. Brought to a house in Bangkok, a Thai man, Samarn Voravong, phoned her parents, Mr. and Mrs. Sok Yorm, in St. Paul, Minnesota, demanding $9,700.The Sok family, who came to the U.S. two years ago, contacted their resettlement agency, World Relief, for help. They continued to receive desperate letters from their daughter in Bangkok, expressing fear for the safety of herself and her child. Interest in the case by Senator Rudy Boschwitz led to an investigation by Thai authorities. A few days after the Sok family paid $400 to the smugglers, they returned her to the border. On May 19, 1987, Thai police raided the extortion den. Sixteen Cambodians who had been kidnapped were recovered, and three Thai men, including Samarn Voravong, were arrested.[42]

Phoeuth's kidnappers were released from prison after less than six months' confinement. In May 1988, the Lawyers Committee received correspondence from the Sok family, including letters from their daughter who is hiding in Site 2 North from her former abductors, who, according to Phoeuth, have threatened to kill her. Although the young woman and her husband are in danger, in October 1988 U.S. officials had thus far failed to grant the family's petition for humanitarian parole.

Protection officers at the U.S. Embassy in Bangkok and UNHCR officials have told the Lawyers Committee that, although there have been many allegations of Cambodians smuggled into Bangkok and held as servants or in brothels, there are few solid clues to work with. In the few successful recoveries, such as the Sok case, information has come from relief agencies abroad. Most cases, however, go unreported because families abroad fear retaliation against relatives still in camps.

5. Land Vietnamese

Vietnamese fleeing their homeland frequently have been raped, robbed and sometimes killed by bandits or Cambodian guerrillas shortly before reaching the Thai border. Vietnamese began

---

[42] See "Immigration Cracks Khmer Smuggling Ring, 3 Charged," The Nation (Bangkok), May 20, 1987.

traveling through Cambodia in mid-1979, during the chaos that followed the Vietnamese invasion.Although dangerous, the land route seemed safer than the journey by boat, where large numbers of people were ravaged by pirates and lost at sea after being rejected by neighboring countries. However, as Ngo Suu, a former political prisoner of Vietnam's "re-education" camps and now a resident of Site 2, informed the Lawyers Committee: "Our miseries are no less than those experienced by the boat people."[43]

Those captured by the Khmer Rouge have been held as virtual slaves -- sometimes as human mine detectors -- or have been pressed into military service. Many others have been detained for weeks or months at KPNLF "hidden border" bases. Some of the detainees have been allowed to go to Site 2 only after relatives abroad have sent ransom payments. Women, sometimes with their children, have been held as sexual objects or "wives" by guerrillas, released only after they are pregnant, debilitated or replaced by a new group of victims. Upon arrival at Site 2, a number of abductees, some as young as 11 years old, have been hospitalized because of repeated sexual abuse. The more fortunate detainees have been transferred to Site 2 after the ICRC has learned of their identities and pressured KPNLF leaders for their release.[44]

Vinh Kham, former deputy leader of the Vietnamese "Platform" in Site 2, explained to the Lawyers Committee that after some abductees arrived at the camp, KPNLF officers have come looking for them, either to sexually abuse them or to demand extortion payment.[45] Asylum seekers held by the Khmer Rouge, such as Vietnamese Montagnard tribespeople, whose release has been

---

[43] From an April 5, 1988 letter made available to the Lawyers Committee.

[44] In many cases, when ICRC field representatives received name lists from released victims, it has taken as many as ten approaches to KPNLF officials and Thai military authorities of Task Force 838 to gain the abductees' release.

[45] Kham was an elected leader of the Vietnamese in Dong Ruk and Site 2 camps between October 1984 and June 1986. He arrived in the U.S. in August 1986.

sought by American sponsors, have been denied access to the ICRC and other international organizations.

Through early 1987, conditions for Land Vietnamese at Site 2 were dominated by robbery, rape and abuse by Thai rangers, KPNLF soldiers and armed bandits.[46] Thai security officials referred to the Platform, the Vietnamese Section of Site 2 South, as a "jail," and considered the residents to be prisoners without legal protection or human rights. Women and young girls, previously traumatized on the "hidden border," were subjected to torment by Thai rangers.

In June 1988, western observers told the Lawyers Committee that, following the Thai government's announcement to turn back all Vietnamese boat people and Laotian asylum seekers, Thai army officials told the KPNLF to "stop all refugees from crossing the border." Site 2 records show that only 30 Land Vietnamese arrived in April and none came through the border in May, 1988. Although most asylum seekers have been reportedly turned back to dangerous areas of the Cambodian interior, some have been held for ransom or for the purpose of sexual abuse. The Vietnamese have particularly been targets of extortion because they are more likely to have relatives abroad who are able to pay a substantial ransom.

6. The Establishment of a Legal Market

Black market trade in border camps outside of UNHCR control has long been an integral means for survival.Recurrent shortages of food, firewood and other basic household goods, and the Thai policy prohibiting camp residents from earning a living, have created a reliance on the black market. Illicit trade has been dominated by Khmer warlords, paramilitary groups and KPNLF officials, who act as middlemen for powerful Thai merchants and military officers. Gunfights sometimes erupted between smugglers and Task Force 80 rangers, who had extracted a tax on goods flowing into the camp. Relief officials reported often hearing gunfire near the area of Site 2 where black marketeers pay "taxes" to the rangers.

In 1987, the Thai government took steps to root out recurrent security problems caused by black market activities in Site 2, permitting a legal market to open in the camp. While Task Force 80 rangers remained in the camp, problems still persisted. In June 1988,

---

[46] See After the Worst, at 236; Seeking Shelter, at 66-67.

the Lawyers Committee received reports that Task Force 80 rangers were enforcing illegal "taxes" on merchants and customers at the camp's legal market.

The opening of a legal market in Site 2 created dissent by local Thai merchants, who had profited from black market activities in the camps. In an interview on January 5, 1988, Kobsak Chutikul, director of the Thai Foreign Ministry's Social Division, told the Lawyers Committee that when plans for a free market were announced, local villagers, who made their living through transporting black market goods into the camp, held angry protest demonstrations. In response, according to Mr. Kobsak, the villagers were "given preferences going into the market."[47]

The establishment of a legal market by Thai authorities is a welcomed effort. Indeed, to date the DPPU has been supportive of the legal market. In a notable reform, in mid-1988, the DPPU, which replaced Task Force 80, expanded the central market, which now covers a 1/2 square kilometer area on the road that divides Site 2 North and South. However, many informed observers believe that, given the size of Site 2 and lack of law enforcement within the camp, the activities by Thai and Cambodian black marketeers will persist. Appropriate measures need to be expanded to ensure that black marketeering is effectively outlawed and punished.

D. Khmer Rouge Camps: Problems of Access

The Khmer Rouge have denied UN and ICRC officials and representatives of international humanitarian agencies regular access to civilian camps in Thailand. There are indications that a substantial number of the 75,000 known residents of Khmer Rouge camps would opt to live in a non-Communist camp if given the choice. There are a number of "satellite camps" along the border where large numbers of Cambodian and, in some cases, Vietnamese and Khmer-Khrom asylum seekers are imprisoned or pressed into labor for Khmer Rouge military units. Additionally, some large camp populations, such as at Ta Luan and O Trao, have been forcibly removed by the Khmer Rouge to areas of conflict, where they have been exposed to shelling by Vietnamese-PRK forces. Those wounded have been denied assistance by UNBRO or ICRC representatives.

---

[47] The large Site 2 population has become recognized by Thai authorities as beneficial yet local merchants. Relief officials express concern that this could inhibit plans to divide the camp into more managemeable and hunane village-like enclaves.

Officials of both FUNCINPEC and the KPNLF have indicated to the Lawyers Committee a willingness to accept people from Khmer Rouge camps. However, except for a few transfers by ICRC during 1988, Khmer Rouge officials appear unwilling to facilitate such transfers. Recently international concern has focused on forced relocation of refugee camp populations under Khmer Rouge control into Cambodia.[48]

Under international law, asylum seekers generally cannot dictate where they are to live in a host country. But the appalling human rights record of the Khmer Rouge should justify an exception. The chilling degree of control exercised over civilians remains obvious in Khmer Rouge camps. Contact with outsiders is restricted, and camp residents who have escaped tell of harsh discipline meted out by Khmer Rouge cadres.[49] The only way to protect the human rights of the inhabitants may be to move them to another enclave not under Khmer Rouge control.

1. UNBRO Access

Those UN officials who distribute aid must monitor that distribuion to ensure that the humanitarian purposes of the aid is achieved. Khmer Rouge officials have given UNBRO access to the 33,000 residents of Site 8, the largest of the Khmer Rouge camps inside of Thailand, located some 50 miles south of Site 2. The Khmer Rouge, however, have stubbornly resisted the presence of international agencies in five other UNBRO-supplied camps located in remote areas along the border, Huay Chan, Na Trao, O Trao, Bo Rai and Ta Luan. Denial of contact with the civilian populations in these "closed" camps has raised suspicion that donated food may be misused. Rare head-counts in some camps by relief officials have uncovered cases of severe malnutrition.[50]

Since Khmer Rouge civilian camps were moved into Thai territory following the 1984-85 Vietnamese-PRK offensive, UNBRO

---

[48] See *Seeking Shelter*, at 74-77.

[49] See *Seeking Shelter*, at 67-79.

[50] See "Ghosts from the Past", *Asiaweek*, July 29, 1988.

has attempted to use the threat of aid cutoffs to obtain access to the camps. Such threats, however, have not always proved successful. On May 1, 1988, UNBRO officials terminated delivery of food supplies to Huay Chan, a camp of 9,000 civilian residents located in the mountainous northern sector. Two years of negotiations with Khmer Rouge leaders to allow international relief workers into the camp and to permit UNBRO officials to verify that food was distributed to noncombatants proved fruitless. More recently, Khmer Rouge authorities dismantled the camp and moved its residents to other Khmer Rouge-administered settlements in the same area. UN officials maintain that they will remain ineligible for international relief.

Khmer Rouge officials have repeatedly blocked medical programs offered by international agencies in Khmer Rouge camps. Cambodians who have spent considerable time under Khmer Rouge control, before and after the Vietnamese invasion, have told the Lawyers Committee that Khmer Rouge officials deny residents access to Western-run medical facilities operating inside the camp. For example, on August 21, 1988, in Bo Rai, a woman who was eight months pregnant was seriously wounded in shelling. ICRC was denied access to treat the woman and she allegedly died on September 4, 1988. In August 1988, ICRC requests to transfer two children suffering from cerebral malaria in Bo Rai and Ta Luan camps were refused. In another case, in mid-1988, a female tuberculosis patient was refused evacuation, and instead was put under house arrest.[51]

ICRC officials state that, most often, the only medical cases permitted transfer to Khao I Dang hospital from remote Khmer Rouge camps are already moribund and die shortly after admission to the hospital. At times Khmer Rouge officials tell ICRC staff that patients refuse evacuation "because everyone dies." The ICRC has expressed concern that such a distortion of facts is being used by the Khmer Rouge to discredit international medical programs among the camp populations.

Residents of Khmer Rouge camps are also denied access to education programs. Except for a small education effort in Bo Rai,

---

[51] The denial of access to medical care has at times caused minor illnesses to develop into serious medical problems, particularly in cases involving the elderly and young children. Reports out of Site 8 indicate that hospital patients cannot seek treatment directly, but must be selected by Khmer Rouge officials.

43

none of the other "closed" camps permit education programs. Instead, young children are given indoctrination and military training by Khmer Rouge cadres.

The ICRC has joined UN officials to protest access restricted or denied to international organizations and voluntary agencies. In 1987, a letter of agreement was signed by the Khmer Rouge representative in charge of refugee affairs, Sim Son, under which he agreed to provide UNBRO with access to all camps. The agreement, however, did not mention other organizations. The resulting access has proved disappointing at best. The ongoing situation at Huay Chan points to the difficulties in implementating agreements made with the Khmer Rouge.[52] In discussions in Thailand in January and October 1988, ICRC and UN officials emphasized to the Lawyers Committee that proper access to perform their humanitarian services among the entire displaced population along the border is the first step in any effort to ensure protection.

2. Satellite Camps, Forced Labor and Mass Relocations

Representatives of international agencies have voiced special concern about secret "satellite camps" just across the border from Khmer Rouge civilian populations inside Thailand. ICRC is denied access to these camps, which are known to be training and logistics bases for Khmer Rouge combatants. A substantial civilian population, including captive asylum seekers, are believed to reside in these camps. Civilian residents of Site 8, especially women, are routinely conscripted as porters for Khmer Rouge guerrillas based in four satellite camps within a kilometer of the border, known by such names as "Site 8 West," "Site 8 North" or Phnum Dey. At least 800 Montagnard tribal people, who had fled persecution in Vietnam due to their previous alliance with the U.S., have reportedly been among those held against their will in such satellite camps. Although their status is currently unknown, their plight was voiced by a group of 200 survivors who escaped from the Khmer Rouge during the 1984-85 border offensive. This group, now living in the U.S., has requested international assistance to release their wives and compatriots being held as virtual slaves and, on occasion, as human mine sweepers. Attempts by U.S. officials to intercede through the Thai military on their behalf have repeatedly failed.

---

[52] See "UN Official Comments on Access to DK Camps," The Nation (Bangkok), September 28, 1987.

Vietnamese have told the Committee that some land Vietnamese who survive passage through Khmer Rouge-controlled areas are held in underground bunkers in the satellite bases. Khmer Rouge officials refuse to acknowledge these captives or that any individuals under their control are held against their will.

International relief staff who work in the Khmer Rouge areas told the Lawyers Committee that Khmer-Krom -- Cambodians who lived in Vietnam -- are routinely imprisoned when they enter a Khmer Rouge zone. Usually, only those who escape from Khmer Rouge prison in satellite areas and come under ICRC protection at Site 8 can be found in a Khmer Rouge border camp.[53] On October 5, 1988, at Site 2, the Committee met Thach Saing, 27, a Khmer-Krom who claimed to have escaped from a Khmer Rouge prison a month earlier. Saing told the Committee that he had been jailed with nine other Khmer-Khrom asylum seekers upon entering Khmer Rouge territory. The jail, an open area surrounded by land mines, located outside of Site 8, held 70 people, including children as young as 10 years old. Captives were made to perform labor and at times carry ammunition for the Khmer Rouge military. Prisoners were reportedly beaten with sticks or guns, some died from sickness without medicine. Saing claims to have escaped when he was assigned to a jail called "the stream on the border," located 4 kilometers east of a Khmer Rouge military position at Khao Din, from which, according to Saing, "no prisoners ever return." Saing talked of doing hard labor while being fed "a handful of rice and gram of salt" per day. He claims to have escaped during fighting and was eventually brought by the Thai army to Khao I Dang.[54]

---

[53] ICRC has an agreement with the Site 8 Khmer Rouge administration that, if Khmer Rouge soldiers seize a patient from Site 8 hospital, the administration must return the captive(s) to the ICRC within 24 hours. During the Committee's October 5, 1988 visit to Site 8, a Khmer Khrom woman who had escaped from the border was in the hospital under ICRC protection.

[54] Interview of Thach Saing through a translator by Al Santoli, Site 2, October 5, 1988. Although the account is difficult to verify, informed observers who have been in Khmer Rouge areas have heard of a jail in the Khao Din area and a "border stream" can be found on maps.

The population of the satellite bases remains largely unknown. Mysterious mass relocations at Site 8 and other Khmer Rouge civilian camps have caused relief agencies and Western diplomats to speculate that Khmer Rouge officials, with Thai complicity, have arbitrarily shifted groups of civilians for military or political reasons.

The movement of camp inhabitants, including civilians, by the Khmer Rouge has a long history. According to UNBRO reports, during the period of January 13-15, 1987, approximately 1,683 residents of Site B were moved to Na Trao, some 150 miles north. Only 413 of the residents of Na Trao were males; it is believed that the women were moved to serve as ammunition porters. The transfer coincided with increased PAVN buildup across the border and intensified clashes in the northern sector.[55]

During mid-1988, approximately 7,000 residents disappeared from Khmer Rouge-controlled Ta Luan camp in southeastern Thailand. In October 1988, UN officials reported that only 2,000 people, many of them elderly or disabled, remained in the camp. The majority of the population had been moved into war zones where they are exposed to artillery shelling, mines and a high risk of malaria.[56] Similar evacuations were reported at northern Huay Chan and Na Trao camps.[57]

A handful of Cambodians who have escaped from Site 8 to Site 2 have told of Khmer Rouge conscription of camp residents to serve as military porters. See Rodney Tasker, "Restless Refugees," Far Eastern Economic Review, July 9, 1987. See also Seeking Shelter, at 72-74; After the Worst, at 191.

[55] See Michael Adler, "Refugees Move Said to Strengthen Khmer Rouge Warlord," Agence France Presse Dispatch, February 11, 1987.

[56] See "U.S. Assails Khmer Rouge Over Refugee Treatment," New York Times, October 23, 1988.

[57] See Binu Thomas, "Ghosts from the Past," Asiaweek, July 29, 1988. Relief officials report that residents transferred from Site 8 to Na Trao in early 1988 were isolated from the camps' original inmates lest they "corrupt" them.

Press reports after the Lawyers Committee trip to Thailand indicate that the movement of Cambodian civilians out of refugee camps in Thailand to combat areas near the Thai-Cambodian border has stepped up.[58] It is estimated that, as of mid-November 1988, Khmer Rouge guerrilla groups moved at least 15,000 Cambodians under Khmer Rouge control to within a few miles of the border. (There are approximately more than 60,000 Cambodians under Khmer Rouge control.) At the border, Cambodians are within easy range of Vietnamese-PRK shelling and are consistently denied medical care or any form of assistance from UNBRO, ICRC or other agencies. In December 1988, international relief officials reported that the relocated Ta Luan civilians were suffering heavy casualties from continual Vietnamese-PRK artillery attacks. One Cambodian source estimated as many as 400 wounded in need of medical attention.[59]

Persons conscripted to carry Khmer Rouge guerrilla supplies into Cambodia have fallen victim to land mines, ambushes by Vietnamese soldiers or malaria and other illness. There are at least 1,000 amputees in Site 8 who are land mine casualties.[60] Relief officials report that traumatic casualties languishing in Bo Rai and Ta Luan camps have been denied Khmer Rouge permission to transfer to ICRC hospital facilities at Khao I Dang.[61]

To maintain its ongoing war effort and discipline among civilians and soldiers, the Khmer Rouge has executed civilians and army deserters. According to a former Khmer Rouge porter who

---

[58] See Steven Erlanger, "Khmer Rouge Moves Cambodians by the Thousands to Combat Area," *New York Times*, November 13, 1988.

[59] See "Kampuchea Continues Shelling," *Bangkok Post*, December 4, 1988.

[60] See Barbara Crossette, "Where Pol Pot Rules: How Heavy a Hand?" *New York Times*, June 1, 1987.

[61] See Binu Thomas, "Ghosts from the Past," *Asiaweek*, July 29, 1988.

escaped to Site B in early 1987, three females who attempted to escape from Cham Krahom guerrilla base in the northeast were executed after being caught.Another female porter was reportedly executed for trying to sneak away to marry a Khmer Rouge soldier.[62]

During 1988, two army deserters were allegedly executed. The first incident occurred during an early evening in April, when 20 to 30 Khmer Rouge police surrounded the hut of a 27-year-old man who lived with his wife and her three children. According to eyewitnesses, when the man, a deserter from the Khmer Rouge army, did not answer police shouts, they fired three warning shots into the hut. The police moved in after the wife and children pleaded to be allowed out. The police then took the man outside of the hut and shot him in the stomach, heart and head. The body was cremated by the Khmer Rouge early the following morning before international relief staff entered the camp.In the second incident, on July 8, 1988, a man who balked at returning to the Khmer Rouge army was executed by being shot in the back of the head near the camp fence, where the body was left, reportedly as a warning to other deserters. Subsequently, the Khmer Rouge administration denied that the incident occurred. However, camp residents informed international agency staff where the body was buried. Although it is difficult to collect detailed information because of Khmer Rouge discipline and fear among camp residents, a number of Cambodians who have escaped from Site 8 confirmed that soldiers who won't go back to the army to fight are executed.

---

[62] See Murray Hiebert, "Caught in the Middle," *Far Eastern Economic Review*, March 19, 1987.

3. Site 8

Site 8, with some 33,000 residents, is the largest and most accessible Khmer Rouge-controlled border camp.Located around 90 miles south of Site 2, the camp covers an open field near the Thai village of Ta Ngoc, at the base of the rocky artillery-scarred cliffs of the Mamuong mountains, that have been the site of numerous border battles. Shelling is a constant fear of camp residents. Relief workers reported shelling just south of the camp during the last week of September, 1988. During the Lawyers Committee visit to Site 8 in early October 1988, the rumble of artillery across the border could be heard in the camp. Relief workers told the Lawyers Committee that the deep seated fear of shelling is manifested by the chronic insomnia reportedly suffered by children.

During the October 1988 visit to the camp, the Committee observed an eerie silence among camp residents, even during mid-day rice distribution. Although Site 8 is known to be the most "liberal" of Khmer Rouge communities, recent escapees told the Committee that residents are restricted from communicating with outsiders or foreign visitors. Even communication with neighbors is considered dangerous due to presence of Khmer Rouge informers. Infraction of rules is punished by "reeducation" and minor infractions are punished by jail inside the camp. However, a number of people have reportedly "disappeared" from the camp for disobeying camp rules. Jails located outside Site 8 are known as Pluon Chai, Phnum Dey and Khlong Nam Soi (near the Khmer Rouge Khao Din military area); few have returned or escaped from these jails. Additionally, some executions of military deserters have occurred in camp.[63]

A limited number of international officials are permitted to work in the central area of the camp.[64] However, their contact with camp residents appears to be restricted. The ICRC has built a small "Tracing Center" in order to locate family members separated by war and displacement. Although Khmer Rouge policy discourages transfer

---

[63] Interviews of former Site 8 residents in Site 2 and international relief workers in Aranyaprathet by Al Santoli, October 3-5, 1988.

[64] The few international agencies present in Site 8 include UNBRO, ICRC, and a medical facility run by CAMA.

of residents to non-Communist camps, since the August 1988 replacement of Thai Task Force 80 with the DPPU on the camp's perimeter, some 15 to 20 Khmer-Khrom and 10 Cambodians have been transferred for family reunification through the ICRC. The ICRC also brings intercamp correspondence to the camp; however, the Khmer Rouge does not permit a post office to function in the camp or mail to be directly distributed to camp residents. Observers contend that the Khmer Rouge continues a campaign of "disinformation" in order to encourage residents "to keep up the war effort."

The DPPU at Site 8 now deploys a team of 67 persons, including six officers and 12 female volunteers. Relief workers claim that the DPPU has been a welcome change from the rangers, who, previously "had rivalry with the Khmer Rouge police over smuggling activities" and sometimes "robbed camp residents and beat them when they boughts goods outside of camp. And charged Thai merchants taxes to sell in camp." The DPPU has encouraged Khmer Rouge administrators to allow residents to buy from Thai merchants at the fence, and have advocated the development of a legal market. Relief workers claim that the growing black market in the camp, where some people sell their "barely standard" food rations, has "harmed nutrition conditions" for some families.The camp's DPPU commander, Prawing Singnarong, told the committee that since he arrived in mid-June, he has explained "the need to coexist" with Khmer Rouge administrators to "create order in the camp."[65] Prawing and relief agencies claim that actions by DPPU personnel to assist camp residents during July and August shelling incidents has gained the trust and respect of the camp leadership.

The sometimes uneasy relationship between the DPPU and Khmer Rouge soldiers was highlighted during an incident in which the DPPU was attacked by Khmer Rouge soldiers. On September 21, 1988, a group of Khmer Rouge soldiers from a nearby military camp attacked a DPPU post at Site 8 with a heavy volume of rifle and rocket-propelled grenade fire. The attack followed a dispute over smuggling on the border between Thai rangers and Khmer Rouge troops. The DPPU reported no casualties from this incident. Some Khmer Rouge soldiers patrolling the area near the camp periodically fire their rifles in the air, presumably to remind camp residents of their power.

---

[65] Interview of Prawing Singnarong by Al Santoli, Site 8, October 5, 1988.

4. Denial of Transfer to Non-Communist Camps

Beginning with the arrival of Cambodian asylum seekers in Thailand in early 1979, Thai authorities have tolerated and at times enforced Khmer Rouge control over unwilling civilians. Some inhabitants who escaped Khmer Rouge labor camps have been handed back to the Khmer Rouge by Thai authorities. The Lawyers Committee has received reports that Thai border security forces continued throughout 1987 to transport newly arrived asylum seekers to Khmer Rouge camps. The Committee and other international agencies have asked the Thai government to moderate their policy toward civilians who wish to leave Khmer Rouge camps.[66] Thus far, as the Khmer Rouge remains the most effective "buffer" guerrilla force along the border, there has been no significant change.

Cambodians have had few, if any, opportunities to be transferred to non-communist camps. The last significant opportunity for a Cambodian civilian population under Khmer Rouge control to transfer to a non-Communist settlement occurred on May 24, 1983. At that time, before Khmer Rouge troops were able to halt the movement, approximately 2,700 civilians out of 20,000 residents of the Phnom Chat camp, displaced by a PAVN attack, chose to defect through UNBRO and ICRC. During mid-1988, approximately 150 Khmer-Khrom (Cambodians of Vietnam citizenship) were transferred from Site 8 to Site 2. This transfer, however, appears to have been an isolated incident. Through October 1988, no significant transfer of Cambodian nationals has occurred. Based on interviews with former residents of Khmer Rouge camps and brief exchanges with some residents inside Site B, it would appear that many Cambodians would choose to live in non-Communist camps if given a choice. Most Cambodians lost many family members during four years of brutal Khmer Rouge rule. And today, even though the outward expression of Khmer Rouge fanaticism has been supplanted with some free-market activity in the accessible area of Site B, few observers or camp

---

[66] In a January 1987 interview with the Lawyers Committee, Thai Foreign Minister Siddhi Sawetsila indicated that Thailand did not wish to create dissension within the CGKD coalition by transferring civilians from one faction to another. In May 1988 discussions with informed Western officials, the Committee was told that Thai policy reflected the People's Republic of China's concern that the Khmer Rouge maintain a viable civilian population for political and manpower reasons.

residents are convinced that the Khmer Rouge have truly liberalized. Ominously, in April 1988, an "eight-point order" issued by the Khmer Rouge at Site B warned that the safety of camp residents who spoke against the Khmer Rouge would not be guaranteed. Involuntary stay is a central aspect of life in Khmer Rouge camps. In late 1986, during a tour of Site 8, Donald Scott, a member of the Board of Directors of Refugees International, a U.S.-based agency, on a private visit was approached by a Cambodian woman of Vietnamese nationality. With her were her two Amerasian children, fathered by an American serviceman with whom she had lived in Saigon. The small family fled Vietnam with hope of finding the father in the U.S. They were intercepted at the border by Thai police who refused to grant their wish to live in a non-Communist camp and were brought to Site 8. The ICRC was never contacted. Scott reported their presence in Site 8 to U.S. embassy officials. But the woman and her children reportedly have disappeared from Site 8. In June 1988, ICRC negotiated release of approximately 150 Khmer-Krom from Site 8 the Amerasian family was not among them.

E.   Khao I Dang: Relocation to the Border

On December 29, 1986, the Royal Thai Government officially announced that Khao I Dang would be closed within two days. The government stated that camp residents would be moved to the border in a phased program.[67]

The closing of Khao I Dang represented a harsh blow to Cambodians who did not wish to align themselves with a particular political faction, as well as those seeking resettlement. The camp, outside the resistance Coalition's control, has served as transit point for most of the 210,000 Cambodians who have found new lives overseas. Khao I Dang is the only camp where Cambodians are under UNHCR care and are permitted to be interviewed for resettlement abroad. In addition, Khao I Dang is located further from the border than any of the other camps in Thailand. Khao I Dang thus has represented an oasis of hope for a generation of Cambodians who have endured 20 years of war, brutal repression and exile.

Thailand's decision to close Khao I Dang was based on three interrelated concerns. First, the decision reflected Thailand's dissatisfaction with third-country resettlement of Cambodians, which fell sharply in recent years. Thai officials, such as former NSC

---

[67] See *Seeking Shelter*, at 95.

Secretary General Prasong Soonsiri, have pointed to "compassion fatigue" in the West. Resettlement countries, including the U.S., have added restrictions to processing procedures that limit admissions criteria.

Second, the Thai government believed that the camp continued to serve as a magnet for Cambodians who hope to emigrate, despite Thai policy to encourage asylum seekers to support the resistance and accept eventual repatriation. In a January 5, 1988 discussion in Bangkok, Sp. Col. Sanan Kajornklam, director of the Supreme Command's Joint Operation Center, told the Lawyers Committee that Khao I Dang's close proximity to the border made it extremely difficult to maintain "proper security" for the camp, whether intruders be bandits or illegal asylum seekers.

Third, the Thai government intended to transform the camp into a training and educational center for border Khmers to learn skills before repatriation to Cambodia in case of a political resolution of the ongoing Vietnamese occupation. Despite Thailand's decision to close Khao I Dang, the Thai government has allowed the camp to remain open until vacillating Western countries clarified their refugee resettlement policies and had sufficient time to interview applicants. In July, 1988, however, Thai authorities announced that all processing at the camp must be completed by October 31, 1988. Thereafter, 12,000 to 14,000 camp residents were to moved to camps along the border.

While the Thai government's decision to close Khao I Dang and move long-time residents back to the border initially provoked strong opposition by international humanitarian organizations and some governments, the October 31 deadline nevertheless appears to have been accepted in Bangkok by UNHCR and Western embassies. At the same time, concern over the future of this population nonetheless remains. The UN Secretary General in an Aide-Memoire dated January 29, 1987, which was provided to Thailand's Permanent Representative to the UN, expressed his concern about the population of Khao I Dang and the choice of a safe location to move the camp's inhabitants. Additionally, there is widespread concern that the political neutrality of Khao I Dang residents could not be guaranteed at border camps, such as Site 2 or Site B.

1. Longstayers, Ration Cardholders and Illegals

In late September 1988, the official population of Khao I Dang was close to 17,000. This population consists of three categories, "Longstayers," "Ration Cardholders" and "illegals." "Longstayers" --

also known as "KD Cardholders" -- consist of individuals who entered the camp prior to August 1984 and number around 10,500 people. "Ration Cardholders," numbering approximately 7,000 people, are those who entered the camp between August 1984 and October 1985. The most serious protection problems are suffered by the "illegals" population, estimated to number approximately 4,500 people. The Ration Cardholders, like the Longstayers, are considered refugees and thus have access to resettlement. The U.S. Joint Voluntary Agency (JVA) began screening Ration Cardholders for U.S. INS immigration status interviews in early 1988. The process is expected to last for several months.

In contrast, the illegals in Khao I Dang are not given access to resettlement abroad. This group is divided into approximately 3,000 people who have registered with the DPPU and some 1,500 people who are unregistered and remain in hiding in the camp. Under Thai deterrence policy, illegals in Khao I Dang are ineligible for food rations or medicine in the camp. UNHCR, however, provides water for sanitation purposes and will provide medical services if they seek assistance. Relief officers express concern about the nutrition and health needs of this population.

Despite the announced closing of Khao I Dang and deprived conditions, numerous Cambodians have continued to enter the camp illegally. Some come directly from Cambodia or from Site 2, while others have lived in Thai villages for long periods. A substantial movement of Cambodians from Site 2 to Khao I Dang was facilitated by members of Task Force 80 during May and June 1988. According to relief workers at Site 2, rumors circulated in the camp that illegal residents of Khao I Dang were about to receive residency cards and qualify for resettlement. At the same time, Task Force 80 military trucks were seen illegally transporting Site 2 residents to Khao I Dang, reportedly at the price of 150 baht ($60) per head. Other Site 2 residents were seen traveling to Khao I Dang on the back of rangers' motorcycles in broad daylight. Seasoned Western observers told the Committee that the rangers "were extracting the last pound of flesh" from desperate Cambodians before Task Force 80 was replaced by the DPPU in July and August 1988.[68] These corrupt practices were ended with the installation of the DPPU.During the Lawyers Committee's October 3, 1988 visit to Khao I Dang, the camp's DPPU commander, Anuphan Patomchai, said that with a skeletal force of only 29 security

---

[68] Interviews of relief workers by Al Santoli, Thailand, May-October, 1988.

personnel to monitor the camp's 35 perimeter posts, "the major problem is people still sneaking into the camp at night."[69] The Thai government is attempting to deter smuggling by imposing a five-year jail sentence for Thai nationals who accept money from Cambodians for passage to Khao I Dang. DPPU policy for apprehended illegal entrants is to hold them in the camp's jail compound until UNHCR and ICRC can arrange to take them to the border camps. During the Lawyers Committee's visit, 34 undocumented Khmer were held in the jail, including 10 small children. Heads of family interviewed by the Committee claimed that they were attempting to seek reunification with surviving family members in the West. All had been brought by smugglers from Site 2.

The plans for moving the illegals to the border have vacillated over time. Those registered are promised to be eventually moved to their choice of Site B, Site 8, Site 2 or its adjacent UNHCR facility called Ban Thad. Although in December 1988, western diplomats reported that the registered illegals would be moved to Site 2. Those unregistered, who maintain hope that Khao I Dang will remain open, are also scheduled to be returned to the border to an undetermined location.

The Lawyers Committee reiterates the importance of the ongoing provision of protection to the Khao I Dang population. With camps such as Site 2 already overcrowded, it is imperative that living conditions and security provisions in all camps be upgraded and the civilians moved away from danger.

F.   Task Force 80 and The DPPU

In April 1988, the Thai Supreme Command, the senior military authority responsible for border security, announced the formation of a special unit to guard the perimeter of the eight Cambodian civilian camps under UNBRO supervision, as well as the UNHCR's Khao I Dang and Ban Thad facilities. The new security force, the DPPU, was created after recurrent abuses by the rangers and in response to requests by UNBRO and other agencies for an upgraded protection system.

---

[69] The DPPU staff was scheduled to be expanded during October 1988 with recent graduates from the DPPU training center. Internal camp security is provided by a security force   made up of Cambodian camp residents.

55

1. Ranger Abuses

From 1980 to August 1988, a Thai army unit, Task Force 80, directed border camp security. The rangers, an all male paramilitary force dressed in black and carrying M-16 rifles, were originally recruited as village defense forces against Communist insurgents in the 1970s. The inherent bias of this poorly trained unit was plainly apparent from the outset. As the director of the Thai Foreign Ministry's Social Division, Kobsak Chutikul, told the Lawyers Committee, "After the 1978 Vietnamese invasion of Cambodia, they were trained to prevent incursions along the border. Therefore, their attitude toward refugees is one of suspicion."

Some rangers have performed heroically -- at times giving their lives -- to protect border camps from the Vietnamese army or Cambodian bandits. However, many others habitually beat, robbed, raped and even killed camp residents.[70]

On July 31, 1987, two widely witnessed crimes by rangers occurred. A disabled Cambodian man and his pregnant wife were shot dead by a drunken ranger as he attempted to rape the woman. The couple were just outside of the camp perimeter gathering firewood when they were attacked and consequently killed by the ranger. In an unrelated incident, another ranger threw a grenade into a camp marketplace. When Task Force 80 officials were reluctant to apprehend the grenade thrower, UNBRO registered protests. In response thereto, Task Force 80 ordered "limited access", temporarily denying access by relief workers to Site 2, banned the use of bicycles by residents inside the sprawling camp and promised more severe retaliation against camp residents if the protests by relief workers did not subside.Subsequent inquiries by UN agencies following the July 31 incidents led to what UN officials describe as an "encouraging" reaction by Thai civilian and military authorities. In a letter to UN officials, the Secretary General of the National Security Council, Suwit Sutthanukun, made clear that "alleged perpetrators of these (July 31) murders would be prosecuted by Thai law, and measures have been taken to improve discipline among personnel."[71] Mr. Suwit

---

[70] See *Seeking Shelter*, at 35-41.

[71] Speech by S.A.M.S. Kibria at annual Conference of CCSDPT in Thailand, October 9, 1987.

and other Bangkok officials ordered Task Force 80 to discipline rangers to prevent a repetition of the July 31 incidents.

Nevertheless, incidents involving Task Force 80 rangers persisted. For example, in August 1987, a ranger at Khao I Dang, apparently suffering from emotional stress, took two other rangers hostage at gunpoint before killing himself. On October 5, 1987, a drunken Thai ranger shot and killed his Cambodian mistress.

On the afternoon of February 12, 1988, a vehicle driven by members of Medecins Sans Frontiers, a humanitarian medical group, stopped at a Thai military checkpoint outside Site 2. A Thai ranger menacingly pointed his rifle inside of the vehicle and demanded money from the relief workers. After an investigation, Task Force 80 officials claimed that the ranger was drunk.[72] In another incident, on June 11, 1988, a ranger fired his rifle into the ground within point blank range of voluntary agency personnel who were attending to another ranger injured in a motorcycle accident in Site 2. The repetition of ranger abuses prompted Thai Supreme Commander Gen. Chaovalit Yongchaiyudh to create a new management system at the Joint Operations Center (SC/JOC)[73] under a respected veteran officer, Sp. Col. Sanan Kajornklam, to better monitor conditions in the border camps. During the Committee's January 1988 visit, UNBRO officials described a "cooperative" working relationship with Sp. Col. Sanan.

In January 1988, Sp. Col. Sanan told the Lawyers Committee of plans to create a more professionally trained security unit to guard the exterior of the border camps. He said that future candidates for the force must be "good quality people who have had at least three years of regular army or reservist training, including some females."

Although cooperation among administrators improved, relief officials in the border camps reported increased violence by camp

---

[72] In June 1988, relief workers told the Lawyers Committee that intoxicated rangers were frequently seen roaming the camp while carrying weapons, which led to incidents of "unacceptable" ranger behavior.

[73] The SC/JOC has authority over all eight UNBRO camps and Khao I Dang.

security during the first half of 1988.Rangers were regularly reported to be involved in beating camp residents who failed to pay them taxes on market activities or extortion tolls for passing from one area of the camp to another. Mail was routinely opened and remittances from abroad were confiscated by Task Force 80 and corrupt Khmer. A new tactic reported by ICRC in April 1988 was house-to-house raids by rangers who seized jewelry, radios, tape players and other objects of value.Incidents of violence committed by rangers or local village defense forces have also been reported outside of Sihanoukist Site B camp. On August 6 and 9, 1987, two Cambodians who had left Site B to forage or trade were shot and killed by local Thai militia.[74] At Site 8, rangers were involved in sometimes violent smuggling activities, as well as brutality against camp residents, inside and outside of the camp's perimeter.

2. The DPPU

The creation of the DPPU, a specially-trained unit, is part of a program authorized by Supreme Commander Chaovalit and Army Chief of Staff Sunthon Kongsomphong to restructure overall border security. During the Committee's October 3-5, 1988 visit to the Cambodian border, the DPPU Commander, Col. Hath Wirasamrith, described their mandate as, "To increase the morale of the refugees before they return to their country. People at UNBRO have the same idea as ourselves about the future of these Kampuchean people . . . we need to prepare them to [eventually return to Cambodia and] rebuild their country."

The proposal for the DPPU came as a result of discussions with UNBRO to address recurrent abuses by Task Force 80 rangers. During January 1988, discussions with the Lawyers Committee in Bangkok, UNBRO officials and Sp. Col. Sanan Kojornklan expressed satisfaction that the UN, which provides the funding for the unit, would have some role during the mandatory six to eight week training session concerning the DPPU.[75] Gen. Sunthon has announced the

---

[74] See "Extrajudicial Executions of Kampuchean Refugees," *Amnesty International Report*, January 1988.

[75] Reportedly, UNBRO will pay more than 1.5 million dollars to cover the costs of the DPPU for a two-year period. On April 27, 1988 UNBRO gave the Supreme Command $450,000 to cover the initial cost of the DPPU.and children at all DPPU camps. The blue DPPU uniforms are meant to be an obvious contrast to the rangers'

Caption: Cambodian children at Site 2, 1988.
Photo by Al Santoli

Caption: Vietnamese aboard a trawler off Thailand's Trat province. The Thai police boat, at

Cambodians being interviewed by JVA at Panat Nikhom
Photo by Lionel Rosenblatt

Mrs. Rodiana a Thai villager wounded by Vietnamese shelling 1985

Caption: Damage to Klong Yai area by Vietnamese Gunners in 1985. Photo by Al Santoli

Caption: Waiting for water ration - Site 2 - 1988

Khmer Rouge – Photo by Lionel Rosenblatt

Caption: Asylum seekers arriving in Thailand

DPPU training will include some English language classes so security guards "will be able to communicate with relief workers." During the October 1988 visit to the border, however, the Committee observed the need for UNBRO to post liaison officers to facilitate a consistent positive working relationship with the DPPU. Sp. Col. Sanan told the Committee that in order to improve discipline, retired regular officers and sergeants from the army's civil affairs battalion would lead the proposed seven DPPU units, totalling 560 guards. These units, divided into "Moral Support Teams," include a unit of women to deal with rape and other violations against women and children at all DPPU camps. The blue DPPU uniforms are meant to be an obvious contrast to the rangers' black pajamas. And unlike rangers, who were habitually seen inside the camps harassing residents, DPPU personnel are only permitted on a camp's perimeter, except to respond to emergency situations.Internal camp security is charged to Cambodian police under the authority of camp administrators. Relief officials have expressed concern to the Lawyers Committee that, given the history of corruption among KPNLF camp administrators and the severe dictatorial rule in Khmer Rouge camps, it is essential that a specially-trained Cambodian police force be formed and placed under monitoring by international agencies.International relief workers on the border told the Lawyers Committee that the initial presence of the DPPU has been "a welcome change." An UNBRO field officer at Site 2 said that 25% of victims of violence in the camp during June 1988 were caused by Thai rangers. In contrast, in the two-month period that began with the mid-August replacement of the rangers, medical records at the Site 2 South hospital show no violent injuries caused by the DPPU. An UNBRO field officer from the Sihanoukist Site B camp told the Committee that DPPU courtesty has extended to "helping refugees with their bags when they arrive at the camp."[76] In Khmer Rouge-controlled camps, such as Site 8, the DPPU has offered to relay relief workers' concerns to the Khmer Rouge administrators.

As the DPPU guards adapt to the border, relief officials warn that there is a need to watch their activities closely, "to make sure they

---

black

[76] See "Unit Forming to Protect Cambodian Refugees," Bangkok Post, April 12, 1988; "UN Agency to Fund Refugee Protection Unit," The Nation (Bangkok) April 15, 1988.

continue positively."[77] One western official expressed concern regarding reports of body searches of camp residents by DPPU during "anti-smuggling" activities.

Informed western observers claim that the initiative for security reforms is largely due to the efforts of General Chaovalit and his appointed subordinates, such as Gen. Sunthon and Sp. Col. Sanan. Consequently, there is concern that if Gen. Chaovalit retires and Gen. Sunthon or Sp. Col. Sanan are rotated to a new command position, their replacements may not have the same commitments to improving border camp security. An enforceable legal system is thereby essential to guarantee protection.

The Lawyers Committee views it essential that the DPPU and UN-supervised Cambodian police within the camp be able to coordinate the disarming of camp entrants at all hours of day and night. Violators, including camp officials or resistance forces, must be apprehended and held accountable for abuses.

G.   Proximity to the Border: External Dangers

On the night of May 29, 1987, a Vietnamese artillery attack on Site 2 resulted in seven civilians killed and 22 wounded. Rapid evacuation of the wounded to Khao I Dang medical facilities by ICRC staff prevented further loss of life. However, though Khmer administrators had organized the Site 2 South population for immediate evacuation, Thai military personnel initially denied them permission to leave the area of attack.

A post-attack investigation led ICRC officials to draft a letter to Thai authorities, calling their attention to the vulnerability of Site 2. The letter also recalled the January 26, 1987 shelling of Site 2, in the Dong Ruk section, when three people died. ICRC launched a public appeal for combatants to respect the civilian character of the camp. Some observers believed that the attack was a deliberate act of terror against the civilian population. On August 29, 1988, a mortar shell landed in the center of Site 2 South and caused one death and two wounded. Additionally, four shells landed in the area of Site 2 South where expansion of the camp is being constructed. The area south of Aranyaprathet is plagued with frequent shellings. At 6:00 a.m. on August 5, 1988, Site 8 was shelled during a "fierce clash"

---

[77] Interview of UNBRO officials by Al Santoli, Bangkok, September 22, 1988.

between Khmer Rouge and Vietnamese-PRK forces nearby. Two Site 8 residents were severely wounded and later taken to Khao I Dang hospital by ICRC.[78]

Shelling in the area south of Aranyaprathet has also affected Thai villages along the border. In mid-1988, during heavy fighting along the border area south of Aranyaprathet and opposite Chantaburi and Trat provinces, Vietnamese shelling caused numerous civilian casualties in Thai border villages and mass evacuations. On June 23, 1988, Bangkok Domestic Radio reported that the Thai Army's Supreme command documented 109 occasions of Vietnamese-PRK artillery shells landing in Prachinburi Province -- a total of 656 shells -- during the past month, causing the evacuation of more than 1,000 villagers. During this period, one Thai villager was killed and seven wounded by land mines planted in Thai soil. Additionally, the ICRC reported 20 Thai civilian deaths caused by shelling during the month of June 1988. Operation Handicapped International (OHI) reports treating an average 4 to 6 Thai civilian amputee land mine casualties per month in its Aranyaprathet facility. A report circulated by Thai officials at the UN documented 100 incursions across the Cambodian border by Vietnamese forces during July 1988 and shelling incidents resulting in 10 Thai civilian deaths and 35 Thais wounded. Additionally, heavy fighting across the border from Prachinburi to Trat has continued into December 1988.

The Thai government has steadfastly refused to permit the border camp population to be relocated to more secure inland areas, claiming that the Khmer camps face the same dangers as Thai border villages. In January 1988, the Lawyers Committee raised this issue with Thai officials in Bangkok. The director of the Foreign Ministry's Social

Division, Kobsak Chutikul, expressed the Thai government's concern that moving the camp inland would:

> give the impression that, instead of people willing to go back into Cambodia at some point, the movement is now in the opposite direction. The perception of a permanent refugee problem for Thailand would create a

---

[78] See "Refugees Wounded at Site 8," Bangkok Post, August 6, 1988.

lot of [domestic] hostility. And such a move would disrupt the military's border security lines of defense. If the refugees were moved behind the defense line, the army -- which already must cope with a serious sabotage problem -- wouldn't be able to differentiate who was going in and out of Thai territory.

Representatives of international agencies told the Lawyers Committee of alternative proposals, such as relocating Site 2 in a more northerly mountainous and wooded area, in terrain offering better geographic protection from ground attack. Thus far, the Thai government has resisted all such proposals. Instead, Thai officials, such as Sp. Col. Sanan Kajornklam of the military's Supreme Command, told the Lawyers Committee in January 1988 of plans to relocate part of the Site 2 population closer to the border in the area of the former Nong Samet camp, which was destroyed by the Vietnamese army during the 1984-85 offensive.

International agencies raised strong objections to relocating Site 2 residents back in the Nong Samet or Nong Chan areas. Both locations are indefensible barren fields. Additionally, serious protection problems are posed by thousands of land mines that have been planted in these frontier areas.

As a compromise, Thai officials agreed to expand the Site 2 living area. Although less perilous than Nong Samet or Nong Chan, relief officials warn that a number of shellings have occurred in the area designated for expansion, including a recent incident on August 29, 1988.

The civilian population under Khmer Rouge control has been particularly vulnerable to spillover fighting and bombardment. On July 12, 1988, eight shells landed in Site 8, killing four people and wounding 12 others. The incident caused considerable panic in the camp; many of the camp's 34,000 residents scattered toward the mountains.The southern Khmer Rouge controlled camps in Trat province have suffered the brunt of recent spillover fighting. For example, on October 9, 1987, when a number of shells landed in Bo Rai camp and wounded at least six people, the ICRC was denied access to the camp because Thai officials said they feared danger to international personnel. Following the incident, the ICRC made inquiries to the Thai government regarding the obvious lack of evacuation plans and consequent anxiety created among camp residents.

Reports on the shelling or spillover fighting incidents that have affected both Cambodian camps and Thai border villages reveal that evacuation plans are dangerously inadequate. In the event of a future Vietnamese-PRK offensive, civilian casualties could be immense.

In past instances of large scale ground attack or sporadic artillery shelling, evacuation of camp residents has often proved chaotic. Most Vietnamese attacks have occurred between midnight and 4:00 a.m. Lack of coordination between Cambodian administrators and Thai military forces has delayed safe passage from impacted areas, at times causing needless civilian casualties. For example, in the pre-dawn hours of September 28, 1987, Vietnamese and PRK gunners attacked the Khmer Rouge-controlled Khlao Plek community with artillery, rockets and mortar fire. More than 3,000 residents, mostly children and senior citizens, attempted to flee across the border[79] near Bang Tung Kanan, a Thai village. However, Thai troops prevented the fleeing Cambodians from crossing the border.[80]

This incident underscores the urgent need for Thai security forces and international agencies to restructure evacuation procedures for border camps and frontier villages. The evacuation area for Site 8, known as Site 9, is a two to three-hour walk from the camp. Although surrounded by hills, it is within range of hostile artillery.

An evacuation site called Site 3 has been designated by UNBRO and Thai officials in case of an attack on Site 2. However, the enormous size of the camp population -- nearing 170,000 -- which includes a large number of children and elderly, combined with factional rivalries among Cambodian administrators, are inevitable obstructions to rapid and orderly evacuations. Further, Site 3, located six miles from the border and five miles from Site 2, is well within

---

[79] Bombardment of fleeing civilians by PAVN and PRK gunners has been recurrent in previous offensives. In instances such as the destruction of the Sihanouk O'Smach camp and the Khmer Rouge-run Phnom Chat camp, wounded civilians were reported purposely shot by advancing PAVN and PRK troops. See Colin Campbell, "Cambodians Tell of Horror," New York Times, April 14, 1983; Al Santoli, "The New Indochina War," The New Republic, May 30, 1983.

[80] See "Army Halts Cambodian Fleeing Battle," Bangkok Post, September 29, 1987.

the 20-mile range of Vietnamese 130mm artillery. And, the route to Site 3, a forest without a road, will hinder an evacuation, especially at night. Although UNBRO has offered to pay for the clearing of a road to Site 3, Thai officials have yet to approve such plans. In addition, medical evacuation to Khao I Dang during the heat of battle with roads sabotaged or crowded with civilian and military vehicles would be nearly impossible.

V. VIETNAMESE BOAT PEOPLE

In January 1988, in one of the year's most dramatic and far-reaching events, the Royal Thai Government formally announced its push-back policy, in which all boats carrying Vietnamese would be prevented from landing on Thai shores. This serious erosion in principles of first asylum signalled Thailand's abandonment of humanitarian notions and the institution of a harsh new policy towards Vietnamese asylum seekers.

Thai security officers carried out their orders with deliberate and often unmitigated cruelty, ramming Vietnamese boats and firing upon innocent and powerless boat people. Thai fishermen interpreted the push-back policy as a license to rape, rob and murder Vietnamese. Hundreds of Vietnamese have died in the push-backs and incidents of piracy.

Such acts of savagery often went unmonitored and undeterred. UNHCR's access to monitor the burgeoning crisis has been severely restricted by Thai authorities. Reports circulated that funds designated to combat piracy were being used to further push-offs. The year 1988 marked the deterioration of the anti-piracy program.

A. The Push-back Policy

During 1987, more than 11,000 Vietnamese boat people arrived in Thailand, a three-fold increase above the previous year.[81] The large majority of these asylum seekers landed near the ports of Khlong Yai and Laem Ngop on the strategic east coast, adjacent to the Cambodian border along the Gulf of Thailand. The east coast route, facilitated by a smuggling network that transported Vietnamese overland through Cambodia to Kompong Som seaport, became a preferred alternative to the perilous 250 mile journey across pirate-

---

[81] In 1987, some 28,000 Vietnamese boat people reached temporary holding centers throughout the region, the highest recorded number since 1982. By mid-1988, with monthly arrivals averaging more than 4,000 and Western off-take commitments dwindling, approximately 60,000 Vietnamese were held in facilities. They included some 15,000 in Thailand; 25,000 in Hong Kong; 14,000 in Malaysia; 4,000 in the Philippines; 3,000 in Indonesia; 600 in Macau; and hundreds more in Singapore, Japan, China and Korea. Except in rare instances, local assimilation of boat people is prohibited in the region.

infested open seas to Southern Thailand or Malaysia that has claimed countless lives since the 1975 fall of Saigon.[82]

The unanticipated surge of boat people in 1987 coincided with fierce battles in Thai territory against Vietnamese-led Communist forces. The conflicts at Chong Bok on the Cambodian border in early 1987 and in Phitsanoluk and Loei on the Laotian border that carried into February 1988 caused hundreds of Thai casualties and touched off wide nationalistic fervor. Added to the government's security concern was the discovery of a massive black market network into Cambodia and Vietnam operating on the militarily vulnerable east coast.

The syndicates, which arranged kickbacks to Thai provincial officials, transported estimated millions of dollars of consumer items, foods, including some items classified as militarily "strategic," in hundreds of small boats based primarily in Trat. On return trips, the smugglers would bring back gem stones and other exotic products, as well as Vietnamese.[83]

Thailand and other ASEAN governments issued repeated appeals to Western countries to step up resettlement to ease the increased flow, but their calls went unanswered.[84] During a publicized December 27, 1987 visit to Phanat Nikhom, Interior Minister Prachuab Suntrangkon expressed outrage at overcrowded conditions and reports of rampant smuggling in Trat. Besides ordering a police investigation into smuggling activities, Prachuab told reporters that until the population in Phanat Nikhom could be sent on

---

[82] Between 1975 and early 1988, some 700,000 Vietnamese boat people have landed on foreign shores.

[83] Police investigators reported that Thai officials demanded up to 35,000 baht ($1,400) for each group of Vietnamese brought into the province. The Vietnamese, seeking a safer exodus than the pirate-infested south, were willing to pay a steep price -- reportedly $1,500 to $4,000 per person. See "Police to Probe Refugee Smuggling Rackets," *Bangkok Post*, January 26, 1988.

[84] See June 1987 ASEAN Foreign Ministers Conference Joint Communique; December 1987 Communique issued at ASEAN summit in Manila.

to other countries, "no more boat people" would be permitted to enter Thailand. "All vessels attempting to land will be sent back to sea."[85]

Beginning on January 17, 1988, a fleet of navy and marine police vessels were deployed in the area between Klong Yai and Koh Kut Island to intercept boats carrying Vietnamese. Thereafter, Interior Minister Prachuab threatened to "replace any provincial officials who tolerate the influx of Vietnamese." Any boat caught bringing in "illegal immigrants" was ordered confiscated and its owner subject to a $4,000 fine and up to 10 years imprisonment. Crew members also faced prosecution. During the first few weeks of the smuggling crackdown, high ranking officials of Trat province, including the governor and police chief, were replaced, as well as nine other police.[86]

On January 27, 1988, the Royal Thai Government formally announced its push-back policy. Characterizing the asylum seekers as illegal "economic migrants," Prime Minister Prem Tinsulanonda and Interior Minister Prachuab Suntharangkul ordered a fleet of navy and policy boats augmented by "deputized" fishermen to "push out any Vietnamese boat people headed for Thai shores.[87] To publicize this tough new policy, on January 27, 1988, at the Klong Yai port, marine police in Trat deliberately pushed a trawler carrying forty Vietnamese

---

[85] See "Red Light for Boat People," *Time*, January 26, 1988.

[86] See "Police to Probe Refugee Smuggling Rackets," *Bangkok Post*, January 26, 1988; see also "Trat Governor Transferred," *The Nation* (Bangkok), February 5, 1988. Additionally, at least a dozen Thai and Cambodian "fishermen" were ordered to face prosecution. By April, Thai authorities reportedly arrested 44 members of smuggling syndicates. Some Vietnamese and Cambodian nationals with assumed Thai names reportedly acted as contacts for payment from overseas relatives of boat people.

[87] See "Government to Push Back Vietnamese, Lao Refugees," *The Nation* (Bangkok), January 28, 1988. The "push-back" policy, which has also forced those who have landed into unseaworthy Thai crafts and towed out to an uncertain fate on the open sea, extends to the south coast. Through mid-October, diplomats and relief workers in Thailand have consistently informed the Lawyers Committee that "the push-off policy in the South is continuing," as well as continued interdiction in the east. And in accordance with MOI policy, UNHCR protected and anti-piracy officers are uniformly denied access to interview Vietnamese on the east and south coasts.

back to sea. Deputy Permanent Secretary of Interior Somphorn Klinpongsa, who presided over the incident and ordered that boats scuttled before reaching land be "left to sink without receiving assistance."[88] This policy was formalized in a Ministry of Interior (MOI) instruction letter to all provincial authorities signed by Deputy Permanent Secretary Somphorn Klinpongsa dated February 2, 1988.

The government's push-back orders inspired ethnic malice. In Klong Yai and smaller villages, public rallies demanded that boat people be sent back to Vietnam. Thai authorities denied UNHCR representatives access to new arrivals, who were forced into donated ramshackle crafts and pushed out to sea. Approximately 1,600 Vietnamese, already in coastal holding centers before the push-backs began, were denied international assistance. On the water, fishermen interpreted the new policy as a mandate to ram and/or pillage defenseless boat people. Smugglers, fearing prosecution or vigilante attack, dumped their human cargo into the Gulf or near barren islands.[89]

During the first three weeks of the blockade, Thai officials estimated that some 1,000 Vietnamese were forced back to sea. With hundreds continuing to attempt to land, outgoing Trat governor Thongdam Banchuen sarcastically told reporters, "I would like to propose that first we give them warnings and if they keep coming in, we just shoot them."[90]

Thai officials made clear their determination to deny asylum. Interior Ministry's Deputy Permanent Secretary, Somphorn Klingpongsa, in turning down a U.S. proposal, to finance a second camp for Vietnamese boat people, stated, "the government's policy is

---

[88] See "Government Tightening Ban on Boat People," *Bangkok Post*, January 28, 1988. The article documents the MOI policy of "towing all illegal refugees back to sea," which was praised by National Security Council Chief Suuwit Suthannukul.

[89] See permanent Mission of Thailand to the U.N., Release Number 3/2531, "Thai Perspectives on the Influx of Boat People," April 25, 1988. The mission explains in part, "Feeling the world no longer cares, and Thailand will be left to shoulder alone the burden of refugees, the Thai government has taken harsh measures such as pushing the refugees to sea or isolating them on barren islands."

[90] See "1000 Vietnamese Refugees Sent Back," *The Nation* (Bangkok), February 6, 1988.

. . . we don't want our country regarded as a country of first acceptance because refugees could remain for 10 or even 20 years."[91]

Although most westerners were denied access to the areas where the push-back policy was focused, a few observers attempted to investigate and provide some assistance to victims. Relief workers reported that on February 9, 1988, sixty-three Vietnamese were forced from a beach shelter at Mai Rut into three rickety boats and pushed out to sea. Two people who tried to swim back to shore were shot dead.

The UNHCR reported that on January 29 1988, a Thai fishing trawler rammed a boat carrying 22 Vietnamese. The impact exploded gasoline canisters killing seven and causing serious burns in others. Two women were abducted by the fishermen. Only eight of the boat's 22 passengers survived.[92]

Western observers found corpses washed up on beaches and received numerous reports by Thai fishermen of finding bodies off the coast. On February 5, 1988, near Klong Yai, fishermen found an estimated 70 corpses, seven with apparent bullet wounds. On February 2, a Thai newspaper quoted fishermen saying they had seen five overturned boats and 84 bodies near Koh Kong.[93] On February 10, fishermen near Mai Rut saw more than 10 corpses including "some with fresh blood." Near Koh Kut, fishermen said, "We are afraid to go out to sea for fear of pulling bodies into our nets."

---

[91] See "Government Rejects U.S. Refugee Camp Request," *Bangkok Post*, February 3, 1988. In a discussion with Al Santoli in New York on April 11, 1988, Somphorn said, "American people express humanitarian concern. What about Thailand's sovereignty? The West doesn't want the refugees and we don't want to keep them." He suggested an island holding cell outside of Thai territory or that the U.S. position an ocean liner in the Gulf "capable of holding 40,000 to 50,000 refugees for screening. Take them to third countries or send them back to Vietnam or Cambodia, without their having to stay in Thailand."

[92] See "UNHCR Accuses Thai Ship of Ramming Refugee Boats," *Bangkok Post*, February 6, 1988.

[93] See U.S. Committee for Refugees, *Refugee Reports*, February 26, 1988, at 4.

U.N. officials estimated in a March 11, 1988 situation report that the push-offs of refugee boats or intentional rammings by Thai police, navy or fishing vessels caused at least 170 deaths. The total number of victims, however, was estimated by surviving boat persons and relief officials to be much higher because many attacks take place far from the coast where no survivors or trace of those drowned can be recovered.[94]

1. The Islands Crisis[95]

During the first weeks of Thailand's push-back policy, hundreds of asylum seekers were abandoned on a group of 52 barren islands opposite Trat province -- without any food, water or medicine. Of the 52 islands, no more than five are inhabited due to the lack of fresh water. Protection problems on these islands are further compounded by their extreme vulnerability to sea bandits.

Thai officials denied relief workers and UN representatives access to the islands to provide people with food, water or medical care. The scene on the islands was described as "a tragedy of first order":

> lots of refugees, including women and kids, starving, eating leaves to survive. Some local villagers reportedly chasing and shooting the refugees with shotguns. Although some local Thai officials attempt to be helpful, they cannot risk admitting if refugees are in their district. The Ministry of Interior threatens that authorities who fail to push out Vietnamese will be fired on the spot. Villagers who provide aid may be jailed for treason.

Relief workers expressed disappointment that the UNHCR in Geneva and most embassies in Bangkok failed to publicly protest to

---

[94] See Henry Kamm, "UN Attributes 170 Deaths to Thai Refusal of Refugees," *New York Times*, April 6, 1988. The death toll was compiled from local Thai officials and villagers and accounts in the Thai press. Some bodies of victims washed up on the Thai coast were inspected by UNHCR staff.

[95] Lawyers Committee Representative Al Santoli returned to Thailand during mid-February 1988 with a team from the Washington-based U.S. Committee for Refugees to investigate the push-backs and the developing crisis.

the Thai authorities. Concerns raised by U.S. officials regarding the breakdown in protection and push-offs were rebuffed by the Thai NSC and MOI and chastised in the Bangkok press. Thai commentators expressed outrage that while Thailand was expected to bear the weight of the increased flow, the U.S. government was planning to decrease its 1988 resettlement quota to accommodate emigres from the Soviet Union. In a February 15, 1988 interview in Bangkok, Kobsak Chutikul, the director of the Foreign Ministry's Social division, stated that in order to maintain first asylum the Thai government would need long-term "resettlement guarantees from Western countries that incorporate more than just unpredictable one year ceilings."

Appeals by the UNHCR office in Bangkok to the Thai government to reestablish asylum were unceremoniously dismissed. During February 9, 1988 discussions with UNHCR representative Gerald Walzer, Interior Ministry officials refused to consider allowing new arrivals into camps and cynically denied that boat people were abandoned on various islands.[96] Along the coasts, Thai officials incited villagers into anti-UNHCR demonstrations, accusing relief workers of "interfering with the internal affairs of Thailand" and being part of an "underground railroad to destabilize Thailand." Essentially confined in the city of Trat, UNHCR protection officers were prohibited by Thai authorities from visiting the coast or the islands.

The situation on the islands was critical. On Koh Salak, a group of 77 Vietnamese clung to 100 square meters of rock and scrub foliage. Composed mostly of women and children, the group had been without food or water for three days. Their spokesman, Dang Kiet, who had spent years in re-education camps in Vietnam, asked for medicine to treat children with fevers and stomach problems. They pleaded not to let the Thai send them back to Vietnam, where they would face "prison or death."[97] The group, most of whom had

---

[96] See "Government Rejects UNHCR Request on Boat People," *Bangkok Post*, February 10, 1988. Mr. Somphorn told reporters that he responded to UNHCR representatives requests that Thailand accept all Vietnamese refugees into camps for humanitarian reasons by stating: "I asked the two UNHCR officials whether the Thai government has to welcome [the refugees] by putting out a Thai tray when they arrive here."

[97] On July 9, 1988, a spokesperson for the Vietnamese Foreign Ministry in Hanoi said, "It's illegal for refugees to flee abroad. The penal code provides for severe sanctions against those who organize

close relatives in the U.S., had already been robbed of their valuables by "men in Thai military uniforms." Kiet said that although they heard on the radio (BBC or VOA) in Vietnam that Thailand wasn't accepting refugees, "We took the risk because we couldn't live under the Communists anymore . . . especially those of us who spent years in re-education camps."[98]

On Koh Phrao Noi, a group was observed which included 28 children, 25 women and 18 men who had been stranded for five days. A grandmother, who drowned when smugglers pushed them into the water, was cremated on the beach. The men in the group carried documents proving they had been prisoners in re-education camps. Many also carried U.S. government issued Orderly Department emigration letters.[99]

Other groups of Vietnamese scattered on the larger islands of Koh Rang Yai and Koh Kut, nearer to Cambodian waters, experienced severe hardship. Letters from survivors documented the tragic results of Thailand's policy.

Mrs. Phuong Thi Hoang, who fled Vietnam to be reunited with her husband in Virginia and was among a group of 71 on Koh Kut, said, "We have been here for three weeks -- hungry, thirsty. Everyone has been robbed. Seventeen people have died." A youth writing to his father, Vien Thuc Le, in Monterey, California said:

> I came with brother Huynh, but after the late July boat turned over. I have no idea where he is. Please let mother know. I was with 30 people, but only half are still alive.

A young woman, Nhung hi Luu, wrote to her sister in Los Angeles:

> We haven't had anything to eat for five days. Some local Thai people would like to give us food, but the

---

illegal departures." See "Asian Countries Invited to Join Refugee Talks," *Agency France Presse Dispatch*, July 9, 1988.

[98] Interview of asylum seekers by Al Santoli, Shepard Lowman and Court Robinson, Koh Salak, February 14, 1988.

[99] Interview of asylum seekers, by Al Santoli, Shepard Lowman and Court Robinson, Koh Salak, February 14, 1988.

police do not permit them. A Thai navy boat came, but nobody helped us.

The island crisis appeared to peak in mid-February. On February 16, 1988, a young woman and her infant died in childbirth on Koh Chang. Others were deathly sick from malaria rampant on the island. Later reports indicated that some deaths had occurred due to the sickness.

2. Divergence of Policy and Practice

On February 19, 1988, the Thai National Security Council announced that UNHCR representatives could provide aid to the estimated hundreds of Vietnamese through Thai relief personnel, although protection officers would not be permitted to interview arrivals or obtain name lists. A total of 520 Vietnamese, most dehydrated and starving, were consolidated on Rang Yai Island. However, international relief agencies were discouraged from making boat trips to search the islands for other stranded groups.[100] Additionally, the U.S. embassy discontinued searches of the islands.

On April 20, 1988, the Royal Thai government signed a Memorandum of Understanding with the UNHCR in Bangkok. According to the agreement, the Thai National Security Council permitted Vietnamese who had been held in make shift holding centers on the coast since before the January 29, 1988 push-backs began and those stranded on the islands to be moved to Site 2 on the Cambodian border.[101] Diplomatic observers report that the UNHCR-Thai agreement included assurances that the Royal Thai government would moderate its position and allow boats to land again. Following the signing of the agreement, representatives of the Thai government also repeatedly stated, in response to diplomatic demarches that its policy was to allow first asylum to be re-established.

---

[100] See "Relief Supplies Sent to Stranded Refugees," *The Nation* (Bangkok), February 21, 1988.

[101] The agreement also provided that Phanat Nikhom was closed to new arrivals, and the Site 2 boat people were denied resettlement abroad. Additionally, the UNHCR agreed to initiate talks with Vietnam (SRV) on "voluntary repatriation" of the asylum seekers. The Thai government ominously warned in the agreement that "if the situation shows no sign of improvement . . . appropriate measures will be instituted by the Royal Thai Government." See "Press Release No. 5/2531, " Permanent Mission of Thailand to the U.N., April 27, 1988.

Despite the signing of the agreement with UNHCR and assurances of moderation, push-offs have continued and indeed remain substantial. In a thinly veiled statement, on April 25, 1988, the Royal Thai Government announced that coastal security forces had received instructions to re-provision asylum seekers and repair boats before being sent off "for their journey to other destinations."[102]

UNHCR representatives maintain that push-offs, while systematic in February 1988, have declined. On October 7, 1988 in Bangkok, UNHCR representatives Pierre Jambor told representatives of the Lawyers Committee that between February 1 and April 20, 1988, 1,643 asylum seekers in 64 boats were pushed off, whereas 1,355 people (around half stranded on islands) in 74 boats were permitted to land. Following this period, Mr. Jambor advised that between April 20 and August 31, 1988, 655 people in 28 boats were pushed off, and 600 people in 54 boats permitted to land.

But internal UNHCR documentation indicates that between April 20 and June 1988 alone, 665 Vietnamese in 31 boats were pushed off. The discrepancy raises questions about the accuracy of UNHCR public pronouncements on the issue.

UNHCR reports show that between May and August 1988, except for five Vietnamese boats that reached Western oil rigs, a total of four refugees were permitted asylum on Thailand's south coast, compared to a 1987 monthly average of some 180 arrivals. A similar comparison on the east coast shows a sharp drop from an average 1,000 monthly arrivals in 1987 (including more than 2,257 in January 1988) to a monthly average of 102 during mid-1988.

In November and December 1988, during heavy monsoon storms, some exceptions were made, especially for pushed-off boats that repeatedly returned to the coast or crashed into an off-shore oil platform. However, the push-off practice appears to continue for most boats.[103]

---

[102] See Thailand Permanent Mission to the U.N. Press Release No. 3/2531, "Thai Perspective on the Influx of Vietnamese Boat People," April 25, 1988.

[103] See "142 VN Boat People Land in Songkhla," *Bangkok Nation*, November 30 1988; see "57 Refugee Boat Survivors Ineligible for Resettlement," *Bangkok Post*, December 2, 1988.

B. Abuses Committed by Thai
Security Forces

Accounts by survivors received by the Lawyers Committee through their relatives in the U.S. reveal a pattern of murder, sexual abuse and robbery by Thai security forces authorized to "push-off" new Vietnamese arrivals.[104]

Typical of such accounts is the account the Lawyers Committee received from Binh Khac Le. Mr. Le departed the Mekong Delta in Vietnam in a group of twelve -- 4 men, 5 women and 3 children -- in a 16-foot boat on February 20, carrying "little food or water." Five nights later, "exhausted physically and mentally due to thirst, hunger and seasickness," the boatmen they paid dropped them into the water near the shore "despite our desperate protest. We men, who knew how to swim, were able to assist the women and children to a strange and deserted beach."

Cutting a path "through the jungle," the next morning the group came upon a Thai military camp. After the military "searched us rather discourteously" and confiscated all of their belongings, the Vietnamese were fed and became hopeful. "But that night was a nightmare. The men were beaten, kicked and hit with their guns. The women were abused, especially My Linh, who was raped to such an extent she was sick the next morning."

After three days of continual abuse, the Vietnamese were pushed out in a canoe that "began leaking as they towed us out to sea. We tried all ways to scoop the water out, but no avail." Fortunately, another naval craft rescued them and after a day of rest gave the Vietnamese provisions of noodles and water, then towed them back to sea in a stronger craft, "directing us to Kut Island. We reached Koh Kut on the evening of March 3."

Finding a small house, the residents gave the Vietnamese some food but "shooed us away, warning: "if we encountered military or police they would shoot us dead." They fled to a deserted island where they lived on coconuts for four days. On March 12, 1988, the group was discovered by representatives of the UNHCR and brought

---

[104] See June 14, 1988 written Instructions from Trat Police superintendent to various police stations in the province, which transmits strict guidelines ordered by Thailand's Ministry of Interior.

to Koh Rang Yai island where more than 500 Vietnamese survivors were congregated.

In another case, a group of 74 boat people were reportedly shot and rammed by Thai security forces during a push-off from Trat province on June 12, 1988. Mr. Hguyen Van Xich, one of fourteen survivors of the original group of 74 boat people, in a letter to his son in New York, recounted that he was ferried to Thailand with four others in a 15-foot "sampan" ferry from Koh Kong, Cambodia on the night of June 8, 1988. Brought to a small village near Klong Yai:

> The Thai villagers tried to warn us that we would be killed by Thai authorities if we tried to go to the refugee camps. We asked for shelter and were allowed to stay until [police] brought us to the Klong Yai refugee camp in a pagoda on June 11. Altogether there were 74 persons, including 25 new arrivals from Koh Kong [a Cambodian island port] and former Vietnamese army officers, including a doctor.
>
> Before being admitted to the camp, we were interviewed, all personal data taken down. Around midnight, we awakened . . . surrounded by Thai soldiers in Para uniforms armed with M-16s. With anger they said that while we had paid the Vietnamese Communists gold to get out of Vietnam, they had not received a cent but also had the burden of supporting us. They added that they would kill us and take revenge by forcing Vietnamese girls to make love to them. They then pushed us into four small boats and towed us into the open sea.
>
> They stopped and ordered eight young girls onto their ship. They then started to shoot the first boat loaded with army officers, causing it to overturn and drown its passengers. While they were aiming at our boat, a light from the distance directed at their ship. They immediately ceased their fire, but steered their ship full speed in our direction. With all our might, we managed to move our boat out of their way, avoiding collision. We were then abandoned.[105]

---

[105] Letter from Nguyen Van Xich to his son Nguyen Anh Chi Linh in Bronx, NY dated June 25, 1988.

After four days on the sea, the small boat landed on an island in Cambodian water. Xich and the other survivors were later found by a Vietnamese security patrol. Although his son was put in "prison" for the attempted refugee journey, Mr. Xich was returned to Ho Chi Minh City (Saigon).

The Lawyers Committee has received other letters from survivors of similar violent push-off incidents that originated at the pagoda refugee camp near Klong Yai. In an incident that reportedly took place on June 27, 1988, uniformed Thai officials loaded 61 Vietnamese into three small boats and towed them to sea where they opened fire with M-16s into the boats, causing the boat to capsize. Of the 61 Vietnamese aboard these boats, only two young boys survived, who were eventually returned to Vietnam. In another account at the pagoda camp during late June 1988, a young woman was abducted by Thai authorities and 31 people were executed; there were only four survivors. The whereabouts of the abducted woman remains unknown.[106]

During a visit to Trat province in September 1988, the Lawyers Committee heard local reports that the Thai military had conducted push-offs from a temple at Klong Yai and the Southernmost port of Hat Lek.

Abuses by Thai law enforcement officials are pervasive. In another incident reported in the press, a Thai policeman pulled a Vietnamese woman by the hair from the hold of a boat where she was hiding. When the woman resisted, in an action of brutality, the policeman threw the woman's baby son into the water.[107]

Thai police have also treated victims of piracy callously. Five young women, the only survivors of a boat of 80 Vietnamese, after being released by pirates on Thailand's south coast near Pattani, were denied asylum in Thailand. Upon arriving in Thailand on July 1, 1988, the women were abandoned in a forest by three Thai police. After walking to a Thai village where they received assistance from

---

[106] Accounts of atrocities by Thai authorities in Khlong Yai area were reported in a July 7, 1988 letter from Pham Ngoc Chung to his father, Nguyen Duc Doan in Long Beach, California and a July 1988 letter from Vietnam sent by a relative of Tran Van Hien to family in New York, made available to the Lawyers Committee.

[107] See Jon Swain, "The Last Voyage of the Damned," *London Times*, October 23, 1988.

local people, on July 6, they were transported by police to another town from which they were placed in a small boat by Thai police and dropped at the Malaysian border. On July 9, they walked to the Malaysian town of Kelantan, and were subsequently taken to Pualu Bidong camp. International anti-piracy officers in Thailand received no information on their existence until UNHCR interviewed them in Malaysia.

C. Abuses Committed by Thai Pirates

Thai fishermen have interpreted the push-back policy and attitudes expressed by Thai officials and police as a mandate to rape, rob and murder Vietnamese boat people. As a Western official told the Lawyers Committee, "Whenever the Thai government speaks negatively of refugees in public, Thai fishermen turn into pirates and Thai security officials become more brutal." People fleeing their homeland, usually without maritime experience in barely seaworthy wooden crafts, are defenseless against radar and sonar-equipped trawlers that usually travel in packs.

The brutal treatment of Vietnamese boat people has been endorsed at high levels of the Thai government. During a March 11, 1988 meeting with a visiting UNHCR regional official, Mr. Somphorn, in discussing the possibility of repatriating "illegal Vietnamese," threatened that "Thailand may have to send their bodies back to Vietnam."[108]

Mr. Somphorn's words were prophetic. Although denied access to asylum seekers in Thailand, UNHCR protection officers have interviewed survivors of pirate attacks in the Gulf who managed to reach Malaysia. UN reports from July 1988 show 75 Vietnamese who are missing and presumed dead due to piracy attacks. One hundred and forty-eight Vietnamese were reported missing in August 1988 most of whom were last seen in the water following rammings by pirate fishing trawlers, who beat refugees with weapons to eliminate survivors. Among reported incidents, a group of 10 Vietnamese were attacked by a fishing trawler on May 18 where four women were repeatedly raped. On May 20, they were attacked by another fishing vessel whose crew gang-raped the same women.

Piracy has been rife in Asian waters since the advent of seagoing craft. Western records of sea gangs in the gulf of Thailand

---

[108] See "SRV to Consider Halting Refugee Flow," *Bangkok Post*, March 12, 1988.

and South China Sea date back to the records of British explorers in the sixteenth century.

Organized piracy syndicates in the region are primarily involved in smuggling drugs, natural resources and electronic products, as well as raiding oil tankers and other commercial vessels. Other gangs are under provincial crime bosses who also run fishing operations. However, the most endemic form of piracy is committed by private fishermen primarily involved in poaching or bullying rivals. Following the 1975 Communist takeover in Vietnam and the advent of boat people, the level and intensity of piracy grew into an internationally-recognized epidemic.

Records of pirate attacks against boat people were not kept before 1980. Between 1980 and 1983, the UNHCR received reports that 1,376 boat people were murdered, 592 women were abducted and never recovered and an additional 2,283 women were raped -- many of whom were raped repeatedly by pirate crews or passed from boat to boat.[109] UN officials estimate many additional cases are undocumented because all involved perished.

There are no recent records of rammings by Vietnamese or Malaysian boats. "The rammings are always by Thai boats," according to a former UN official. On October 16, 1988, an anti-piracy expert told the Committee:

> The number of deaths caused by rammings are astounding, like nothing we've seen in the five years I've monitored Southeast Asia. The numbers who perish are much higher than the survivors report because many boats are destroyed without survivors to testify.

UNHCR representatives reported that on May 11, 1988 a boat with 79 Vietnamese arrived in Malaysia after being pushed off by Thai forced on three occasions during a month-long period. Between the first and second push-off, the boat was attacked by Thai pirates who watched the marine police tow the boat to sea and patiently waited for the police to leave before attacking. Six women were gang raped.

---

[109] Statistics cited by UNHCR Director of Protection, Michel Moussalli, Speech to Assembly of Maritime Organizations, London, November 8, 1983.

Documented incidents related by survivors reveal a pattern of increased savagery in pirate attacks. Ms. Mi Thi Nguyen, 24, was the only survivor out of a boat of 41 attacked by Thai fishermen on January 10, 1988. Ten women and girls were kidnapped. Eight of the women jumped into the sea in an act of suicide after the pirates threw their children overboard.[110]

Son Minh Do, his wife and four small children were among 24 asylum seekers who fled Vietnam on February 18, 1988. Attacked by fishermen on the following day, their children were among ten children who drowned, all of whom were under seven years of age. Survivors were rescued by a freighter and landed on a Thai island.[111]

On April 22, 1988, a boat carrying 44 Vietnamese was attacked by fishermen who robbed them and abducted five women, ranging in age from 16 to 31 years old. The boat was then rammed and those trying to swim were beaten with poles, resulting in their drowning. Three surviving men were rescued by a passing vessel and brought to Malaysia. The five abducted women were recovered in Malaysia on April 30.

In another reported incident, on May 9, 1988, a vessel carrying 27 Vietnamese was assaulted by a Thai fishing trawler in the open sea on the Gulf. Three women, aged 27, 18 and 14, were abducted. The trawler intentionally rammed the boat, causing it to sink. When the Vietnamese desperately tried to climb aboard the Thai craft, the fishermen hit them with poles and knives. Only two of the 26 Vietnamese aboard the boat survived; they were rescued by a passing ship after floating at sea for almost 24 hours and were subsequently interviewed by UN officials in Kelantan, Malaysia.

In an incident recorded by UNHCR field officers, on July 9, 1988, Thai fishermen threw five abducted women and six children into the sea, where they drowned. This incident was reported to Malaysian authorities on July 11, 1988 by five surviving abductees.

---

[110] See Barbara Crossette, "Thai Fishermen Again Brutalizing Vietnamese Refugees, Survivors Say," *New York Times*, May 2, 1988.

[111] *Ibid.*

Besides brutality at sea, there have been increased reports of abuses by Thai pirates on the east coast, which include the experience of 17-year-old Miss Diem Chi Nguyen.[112]

Diem Chi escaped from Vietnam with her father (a former re-education camp prisoner), her 14-year-old brother, and 12 other people on March 23, 1988. Two days later, attempting to navigate their way across the Gulf, they were surrounded by three Thai fishing trawlers. Diem Chi and five other women were divided among the the pirate boats and gang-raped until past midnight. Returned to the small boat which was tied by rope to a trawler, Diem Chi was again abducted. "Alone on their boat, subject to many ugly and terrible abuses, I cried my lungs out, but they did not have pity."

Around 10 o'clock the next morning the Thai pirates pulled her father and younger brother up to the pirate boat. "My father and brother hugged each other and pleaded with the pirates to permit us to live or die together." Not knowing what became of their boat, for the next five days the Thai allowed Diem Chi to spend daylight with her family:

> but at night we were separated while I suffered tragedy. I tried to stomach everything in order to save the lives of the three of us. My father had to swallow his immense pain. But things did not turn out as we wished. Around 1. a.m. on April 1, the pirates threw my father into the sea. A couple of hours later they threw my brother, who was fortunate to catch hold of a piece of wood and float on the ocean for three days until he was rescued. But we never had news of my father.

> I cried until the next night when we neared a port. But the pirates locked me in a small cupboard for two days without water.

After midnight on April 4, Diem Chi escaped and swam ashore to a Thai port. But instead of finding shelter, the local Thai authorities sexually abused Diem Chi and jailed her for 23 days. Diem Chi was sent to Site 2 on April 27, 1988.

---

[112] A written account by Miss Diem Chi Nguyen was delivered to the Lawyers Committee through her brother, Anh Tuan Nguyen of Buffalo, New York, on June 20, 1988.

In yet another instance, two teenagers, who were among five women gang-raped by pirates during two incidents at sea on March 11 and 7, 1988, described the impact upon themselves:

> Living on the Cambodian border, we sometimes hear artillery and understand that sometimes people have to run when shells land in the camp. Being girls alone without family in camp is very dangerous. We are afraid because we remember our past tragedy. If it happens again we don't know if our minds can bear it.[113]

While incidents of piracy are difficult to document and are frequently unreported, reports of abuses committed against asylum seekers vary. On October 7, 1988, UNHCR representatives for Thailand, Pierre Jambor, told the Committee that while the viciousness of piracy attacks had intensified, between February and August 1988, there were only 11 deaths and 26 rapes due to piracy between April and August 1988, there were no deaths and only one rape.[114] But a press account of a single incident in May 1988, reported that 20 Vietnamese died and six women were raped. According to the report, La Kieu Ly, aged 16, left Vietnam on May 10, 1988. Ly's boat carrying a group of 21 boat people, was attacked and rammed by pirates shortly therafter. Ly and her ten-year-old sister, and four other females from the boat were abducted, raped and finally thrown overboard into the sea. Ly was the only survivor; she was rescued by Thai fishermen and arrived in Ban Thad in June 1988.[115]

Smugglers have also caused the deaths of Vietnamese boat people. On September 26, 1988 in Bangkok, Thai Ministry of Interior officials told the Committee that "the problem with smugglers (of boat people)" includes dropping boat people into the open sea three to five

---

[113] See Letter from Ngo Kin Phuong (aged 16) and Bui Thi Bach Tuyet (aged 17) to Al Santoli, Ban Thad, October 26, 1988.

[114] Interview of Pierre Jambor and Kaiser Zaman by Arthur Helton, Roni Rubenstein and Al Santoli, Bangkok, October 7, 1988.

[115] See Jon Swain, "The Last Voyage of the Damned," *London Times*, October 23, 1988.,

kilometers off the Thai coast which has caused a number of deaths.[116] The deaths caused by smugglers transporting Vietnamese from Cambodian ports to Thailand's nearby east coast has largely coincided with Thailand's 1988 push-back and interdiction policy.

D. The Deterioration of the Anti-Piracy Program

Throughout 1987 -- before the Thai push-back policy began -- UN anti-piracy reports indicate that there were not deaths and 35 missing and three unrecovered abducted women attributed to piracy. However, during the first eight months of 1988, based on survivors' accounts and figures provided by UN reports, the Lawyers Committee has counted at least 530 dead and presumed dead and 24 women who have been kidnapped and whose whereabouts remain unknown. Additionally, survivors have reported abuses committed by Thai uniformed security officials on Thailand's east coast during June 1988 of 109 casualties and 9 unrecovered women. These figures, as well as the examples of incidents of push-offs and piracy discussed above, signal the dramatic deterioration of the anti-piracy program.

In 1981, Thailand initiated an anti-piracy program funded with a $2 million subsidy from the U.S. government. The following year, the anti-piracy effort was institutionalized through UNHCR funding donated by twelve countries, with the U.S. the largest contributor. The program was operated primarily by the Royal Thai Navy, coordinating efforts with UNHCR representatives in Songkhla, on the south coast near the Malaysian border.

The program at first had little success. The anti-piracy unit owned only three patrol boats and two small spotter planes to cover approximately 33,000 square miles of territorial water and to monitor some 50,000 private fishing boats, which are often faster and better equipped than the navy. Nearly 75 percent of all boats that arrived in southern Thailand between 1981 and 1984 were attacked at least twice.

The anti-piracy program, however, began to succeed in 1985 with a shift to a land-based law enforcement strategy. To complement the UN-assisted effort, the U.S. Embassy established a regional anti-piracy unit to serve in an advisory capacity with Thai marine and provincial police. During this period the UNHCR hired

---

[116] Interview of Prapakorn Smiti, Ministry of Interior by Al Santoli, Bangkok, September 26, 1988.

an anti-piracy consultant and assigned a lawyer to the anti-piracy program. When the Lawyers Committee visited Thailand in January 1988, the U.S. embassy anti-piracy offficer, Steve Kraus, explained that the U.S. effort:

> focused tremendous resources on training provincial police. And we have also created radio and TV announcements emphasizing that piracy is unacceptable. Police marching bands, as well as Thai puppet shadow plays and theatre troupes have gone into fishing villages to explain that piracy, like drug addiction and other crimes, should be discouraged.[117]

Increased success in the program was also attributed to prompt prosecution of alleged perpetrators of abuses. Kraus stated that the key factor in cases of arrest and prosecution was the testimony of Vietnamese witnesses. In the past, piracy victims feared retaliation or being held back from resettlement because of lengthy waits before trial. During 1986-87, prosecution and trials were prompt. Hence, "assistance given by witnesses did not slow their resettlement process."[118]

Diligent law enforcement efforts seemed to have led to a drop in piracy. While only 30 suspected pirates were arrested during the first four years of the program, in 1986, 50 suspects were apprehended. Twenty-one of those defendants were found guilty of one or more charges and received sentences ranging from three to 50 years, as well as one death sentence.[119] Wherease 44 percent of the

---

[117] Although the U.S. is still the largest donor to the UN anti-piracy program, the financial help has been reduced significantly. The $1.75 million U.S. contribution in 1987 was reduced to $1 million in 1988. In July 1988, the UNHCR gave Thailand $2.7 million to extend the anti-piracy program, without bringing up reports that the program's assets were being misused to deny entry and push-off arriving asylum seekers.

[118] Interview of Steve Kraus by Al Santoli, Arthur Helton and Larry Eisenstein, Bangkok, January 4, 1988.

[119] See "Court Gives Death Sentence for Piracy, *Bangkok World*, December 13, 1986. The Songkhla provincial court handed down the death sentence to Mesa Sukchan, and 15 to 22 year sentences to Mesa Sukchan's three accomplices for murder, rape and robbery of boat refugees on the high seas during October 1986.

boats arriving in southern Thailand in 1986 were attacked by pirates, 30 percent of the arriving boats in 1987 were attacked.

Relief workers believe that although the anti-piracy program greatly contributed to the decrease in criminal incidents at sea and on the coast through 1987, other factors also contributed to lowered statistics. Informed observers believe that in response to increased prosecution, pirate attacks became more murderous "to make sure that no victims survive to report them."

New escape routes were used by the Vietnamese to circumvent piracy. Beginning in 1984, many traveled overland through Cambodia for a short boat ride from Kompong Som and Koh Kong seaports to Thailand's east coast. By 1986, 2,222 Vietnamese arrived in the east, compared to 1,664 in the south where most attacks have occurred. In 1987, the number arriving on the east coast escalated to 7,847 from 3,348.[120] Most departures were facilitated by well-paid smuggling networks who secured the small groups of Vietnamese from attacks.

Despite such successes in the past, the anti-piracy program virtually collapsed in 1988 with the institution of the Thai push-off policy. Through October 1988, the consensus of relief workers in Thailand was that the UNHCR-funded anti-piracy program is "in serious decline. "

On March 10, 1988, a Western diplomatic source told the Lawyers Committee that with violent incidents of piracy at sea intensifying, "the Thai are enforcing official nationwide policy against boat arrivals more vigorously than in the past." A relief official added:

> It's ludicrous to talk about anti-piracy when the Thai government is doing all it can to prevent boats from coming. Anti-piracy is in shambles, in the east and the south. And international coverage of the coast and the islands is non-existent.

Thai naval and marine forces -- although clearly aware that Vietnamese boat people had been subject to pirate attacks -- have

---

[120] In contrast, Cambodian waters have had a less pervasive history of piracy. UN statistics show that during 1988, piracy was reported by 9 percent of boats interviewed by UNHCR (many pushed-off boats were unable to be seen), up from a 6 percent attack rate during 1987.

towed piracy victims out to sea without asking any questions about piracy. For example, a boat of 22 Vietnamese suffered two vicious pirate attacks in the Gulf on March 1, and 7, 1988, in which 5 young women aged 16 to 29 were repeatedly gang-raped. They were subsequently pushed off the Thai coast on three occasions before being found by the UNHCR on Koh Chang island on March 19, 1988. The leader of the group, Mr. Nguyen Van Tran, who had spent eight years in reeducation in Vietnam, told the Committee: "During the second push-off I told the Thai naval officer, 'I appeal to your humanity to help us.' The officer replied, 'Our policy doesn't give us permission to do that. We just pull you out.'" The Thai authorities reportedly asked no questions about piracy during any of the encounters.[121]

In September 1988, a veteran relief official told the Committee:

> Although publicity is less, the Thais have behaved worse toward the refugees because they know that they can get away with it. No embassies or UN officials forcefully raise the issue that protection is an integral aspect of first asylum.

Attempts at "quiet diplomacy" by UNHCR and other international officials has proven largely ineffective, according to a number of relief workers.

Thai officials have effectively precluded UNHCR from playing an effective role in anti-piracy efforts. UNHCR was publicly warned to refrain from pursuing its protection mandate and threatened that its representatives "may be expelled because they are acting against the interests of the host country."[122] A Ministry of Interior instruction on February 2, 1988, denied permission to UNHCR, other international protection officers and embassy staff to interview arrivals on the coasts or the islands, including those who had been abused at sea. Anti-piracy experts state that the Thai policy to delay interviews for one to four weeks, until after the refugees arrive at Site 2, hinders effective pursuit and prosecution of sea criminals. During a visit to Trat Province and the island of Koh Kut on September 22-23, 1988, the

---

[121] Interview of Nguyen Van Tran by Al Santoli, Site 2, October 5, 1988.

[122] See Letter by former Thai Foreign Minister Thant Khoman in *Bangkok Post*, February 11, 1988.

Committee found that this Ministry of Interior policy was being strictly enforced.

Provincial officials seldom inform UNHCR representatives of arriving asylum seekers. The Trat UN office usually relies upon information from unofficial sources, then approaches Thai officials to confirm reports and request permission to donate supplies and shelter materials. The Committee found local officials reluctant to discuss the arrival of Vietnamese. Villagers on the coast and the island requested assurances that the Committee's team was not associated with the UNHCR and were reluctant to provide information. In fact, the Committee learned that local officials systematically deny the presence of arrivals, which allows push-offs and abuses by Thai police to occur without discovery.

Routine search of the 52 islands of the east coast has not been regularly conducted by UNHCR, relief agencies or U.S. anti-piracy officials since early 1988. During the September-October visit to Thailand, the Committee learned that U.S. Embassy staff had made only brief periodic visits to the east coast since Spring 1988, and virtually no independent searches of either coast or the islands off Trat.

Additionally, there has been an apparent lack of coordination of information between the UNHCR and U.S. anti-piracy programs. When Lawyers Committee delegate Al Santoli arrived in Trat on September 22, 1988, accompanied by a U.S. refugee protection officer, the local UNHCR office told of providing supplies to Thai officials for a group of 73 boat people under Thai custody on Koh Kut island since September 17. The U.S. officer, however, had no previous knowledge of this group.

And in Klong Yai, the port opposite Koh Kut island a district official denied any knowledge of the Vietnamese group. On September 23, the Committee chartered a private boat to Koh Kut, where they found the group which included a number of small children[123] under the custody of Thai marines, who denied permission to visit the group.

----

[123] The Koh Kut group was one of two boats whose passengers were permitted to land on Thailand's east coast and islands during September 1988, totalling 76 people. On October 4, 1988 at Site 2, the Committee interviewed the group's spokesperson, Father Tran Hoang Kim, a Catholic priest who had spent more than 13 years in reeducation camps in Vietnam. He said that a Thai guard told the group, "You are very lucky."

Relief workers in Thailand have expressed serious concern that UNHCR-funded Thai anti-piracy patrol units are now being used to push-off Vietnamese. In June 1988, an informed observer told the Lawyers Committee that some UNHCR officials "are afraid to report the abuse of the anti-piracy assets publicly for fear of losing program funding. Or because the Thai may completely eliminate the program" (which received $2.7 million from UNHCR in July 1988).

On February 23, 1988, a coalition of international humanitarian agencies based in Thailand sent a statement to the U.S. House of Representatives requesting an investigation into the misuse of the anti-piracy program. They quoted an article from a Thai newspaper dated February 28, 1988, which reports, "Combined anti-piracy forces have apprehended 50 boat people illegally landing in Nakhon Si Thammamarat province in three separate occasions this month . . . during a series of sea and air patrol along the Gulf of Thailand."

The Lawyers Committee is concerned about reports from delegates who attended the UNHCR Donors Meeting on the anti-piracy program, held in Geneva in May 1988. UNHCR officials reportedly told the delegates that "there is no evidence of the Thai navy using anti-piracy assets for push-offs." However, according to Thai newspaper accounts[124] and interviews of Vietnamese, it appears that anti-piracy assets may have been used throughout mid-1988.

Concern has also been expressed about plans to abolish a consultant position in the UNHCR anti-piracy program. Currently, the program has a staff of three. While arrivals are down, the reduction in numbers may well be due to push-back practices. More monitoring, not less, may be indicated.

E. Further Erosion of Rescue at Sea

The provision of asylum and the duty to rescue at sea has been further eroded by the harsh demands made by the Thai Ministry of Interior. During the Committee's October 1988 visit, Thailand refused to allow 63 asylum seekers, including 36 women and children, to disembark from a Cypriot freighter that had rescued the group from a sinking boat at sea. The Committee learned that the Thai Ministry of Interior demanded that UNHCR and western embassies specifically

---

[124] See, "50 Boat People Apprehended," *Bangkok Post*, February 28, 1988.

identify where each asylum seeker would be resettled and the date of resettlement before any person was granted temporary asylum.

In Bangkok, Thai Ministry of Interior officials told the Committee that Thailand was taking a harsh position on rescue at sea cases because in the past, "The U.S. doesn't respond unless the refugees have links to the U.S. And Canada and Australia use the 'medical hold' provision of the RASRO (Rescue at Sea) law to keep people in Thailand longer than the (mandated) 30-day period."[125]

Relief officials and diplomats express concern that by capitulating to Thailand's demands, UNHCR officials in Geneva are facilitating the erosion of rescue at sea. On October 6, 1988, a Bangkok-based diplomat expressed concern to the Committee that

> rescue at sea is being seriously eroded. This is the third case since January 1988 where Thailand has changed the rules, and UNHCR has capitulated. In an earlier incident, when a Soviet freighter picked up four Vietnamese boat people, Thai MOI official Somphorn Klingpongsa requested that the ship's captain contact Moscow for permission to take the refugees to the Soviet Union.

By precluding asylum seekers from disembarking from international ships in Thai ports, Thai authorities have in effect discouraged ships destined for Thailand from rescuing people stranded at sea. A two week delay at port, such as in the case of the Cypriot vessel, is extremely costly, may cause the loss of the cargo mission and may subject the vessel to various penalties. Such acts in effect serve as a warning to commercial shipping firms not to pick up refugees if Thailand is their destination.

Customary principles of international law have recognized a duty to rescue those in danger at sea -- a doctrine which is closely related to the principle of non-refoulement.[121] This principle is firmly established in international law and can be traced back to the

---

[125] Interview of Prapkorn Smiti by Al Santoli, Bangkok, September 23, 1988.

[121] G.S. Goodwin-Gill, The Refugee in International Law, at 69 (1983) (and source cited therein); J. Pagash, *The Dilemma of the Sea Refugee: Rescue Without Refuge*, 18 Harvard Int'l L.J. 577, 578 (1977).

Brussels International Assistance and Salvage at Sea Convention of 1910, which was ratified by 63 nations. The great majority of international agreements relating to safety at sea signed after 1910 -- including the 1958 Convention on the High Seas and the 1960 London International Convention for the Safety of Life at Sea,[122] -- have incorporated a provision endorsing the duty to rescue.

F. Phanat Nikhom

Vietnamese arriving in small groups on Thailand's east coast or in larger clusters in boats on the South coast in the past were held briefly in provincial shelters before being transported to the Phanat Nikhom camp. Phanat Nikhom, located 50 miles southeast of Bangkok, is administered by the Thai Ministry of Interior with UNHCR-provided relief assistance.[123]

The camp is divided by a highway into two separate areas, an out-processing transit center and a Vietnamese section. The transit center serves all Indochinese refugees preparing to depart Thailand and includes a six-month English language program for Cambodians and Laotians accepted for resettlement in the U.S. Across the highway is the Vietnamese section, known as "Section C." This area, which is surrounded by a corrugated tin and barbed wire fence, houses Vietnamese who arrived before the Thai government formally instituted its push-back policy on January 27, 1988. Vietnamese boat people permitted entry into Thailand after January 27, 1988 are classified as "illegal aliens" and sent to Site 2 on the Cambodian border.

The Lawyers Committee visited Phanat Nikhom on January 14, 1988. Due to the surge in east coast arrivals, Section C, which was built to temporarily hold 8,000, was overflowing with more than 14,000 men, women and children. The Thai administrator of the camp, Mr. Karan Supakitvilaekarn, told the Committee that waning Western resettlement programs made "overcrowded conditions a serious problem."

---

[122] Pagash, at 579.

[123] The October 1988 population of Phanat Nikhom included: Section C, 7,874; Processing Center, 9,500 (Khmer 2,804; Lao 2,403; Hmong 4,295) and Transmit Center, 1,598 (Hmong 240; Lao 97; Khmer 1; Vietnamese to Bataan RPC 1,206).

On October 8, 1988, the Lawyers Committee again visited Phanat Nikhom and observed that the severe overcrowding in Section C had been reduced, primarily by U.S. resettlement, to a more manageable 7,874 individuals.

Humane treatment, however, goes beyond issues of overcrowding. A clinical psychologist working with UNHCR observed that a more serious problem than crowding in the camp is hopeless confinement. "They feel that there is no escape." In some cases, long-term confinement has led to suicide attempts. On July 22, 1988, a family of 10 "long-stayers" attempted suicide following rejection for resettlement.

Although protection problems in the camp may not be as sweeping as those along the Cambodian border, one specific problem reported by former camp residents and relief officials concerns systematic abuses by the Thai leader of Section C security, Mr. Wanchai Noitoi, known as "Mr. Joe," and his cohorts. Mr. Joe has a reputation for terrorizing and beating camp residents.

In one incident, on August 28, 1988, Mr. Joe beat and kicked Ma Diec Kim. Although Kim's arm was broken during the beating, he was denied medical care and instead was placed in jail. Kim received medical care only after he assured Mr. Joe that he would say that he was injured during a fall.[124]

Mr. Joe's capricious exercise of power was reflected in 1987 reports from relief workers that Mr. Joe had personally "screened out" a number of boat people for transfer to Site 2. A number of these people were reportedly Khmer citizens of Vietnam. The camp's UNHCR representative managed to reverse a handful of transfers where families would have been separated.

Mr. Joe's cadre of Thai deputies and "Aran boys" (deserters from the Vietnamese Army stationed in Cambodia), who are allegedly responsible for "security" matters, have also terrorized and intimidated camp residents.[125] A typical case, that occurred in mid-1987, was

---

[124] Representatives of the Lawyers Committee interviewed Ma Diec Kim on October 6, 1988 in the Suan Phlu Immigration Detention Center in Bangkok, where he was being held for his own protection.

[125] Unlike other ethnic groups in Phanat Nikhom, the Vietnamese have not been permitted to elect their security representatives, who are appointed instead by Thai officials, such as Mr. Joe.

reported to the Committee by a former camp resident, Tran Vinh (alias), 20, now living in New York. Following the sexual assault of a neighbor by the Vietnamese chief of the building's security, two of Mr. Joe's security men, Chung and Long, severely beat Vinh to persuade him to "modify" his testimony before camp administrators. Although the chief was relieved of authority and sentenced to 15 days in the camp's jail, Vinh claims, "Joe's [men] beat me until I passed out. They told me that I had to make a false confession to discredit the woman's story, to make the ex-chief appear innocent, and to put her in jail." When Vinh refused to comply, he was repeatedly harassed by the security men until he departed for resettlement.

In another case that occurred on March 31, 1988, a Vietnamese woman, Ms. Truong Thanh Phuong, 28, died after a rape by an unidentified person under suspicious circumstances. Although she was diagnosed by a doctor in the camp as having "possible brain trauma" following the attack, the Thai medical report stated that her death was caused by "rabies." A subsequent investigation by Thai camp authorities failed to find the rapist.

A number of camp residents have told of all-day orientation assemblies conducted by "Joe and his men," where threats were made against reporting security incidents to UNHCR or other camp authorities. Additionally, some camp residents reportedly have had to pay bribes to security guards for permission to live near relatives or friends.

The Lawyers Committee has received reports that UNHCR has been denied access to the camp's jail, where a number of beatings have allegedly occurred. Victims have been reportedly intimidated by camp security guards to prevent them from reporting abuses to UNHCR or relief workers in camp. Additionally, attempts by UNHCR to implement a procedure involving the "victims of violence report form" used in the border camps has been reportedly rejected by the Thai Ministry of Interior.

Although Mr. Joe was reportedly transferred for disciplinary reasons in October 1988, the Committee received reports that he was back in Section C. during November and December following the arrival of a new camp commander.

G. Ban Thad

The bamboo hut "boat people annex" known as Ban Thad, is located in a fenced-in area in the southern most area of Site 2. It is separated by a 500 meter open field and Thai DPPU guard posts from the Cambodian Rithisen area and the Land Vietnamese Dong Ruk Platform and Section 5 areas. Built on an abandoned rice paddy without trees for shade, the area quickly floods during monsoon rains and becomes oven-like during the dry season.

Ban Thad was constructed under UNCHR supervision in late Spring 1988. The relatively few Vietnamese who have reached land or offshore oil rigs since April have been sent to Ban Thad. Ban Thad is administered by the UNHCR, which has 24-hour access to this section of the camp.

Ban Thad was constructed under the terms of a Memorandum of Understanding signed in Bangkok on April 20, 1988, between the Thai government and the UNHCR, which arranged for the protection and shelter of boat people permitted to land in Thailand. Around 2,000 asylum seekers held in temporary centers on the east and south coast since before the January 29 push-back policy were to be moved to an "annex to be constructed" at site 2. However, these Vietnamese and subsequent new arrivals were classified as "illegal immigrants" and deemed ineligible for resettlement. In addition, UNHCR agreed to pursue "durable long-term solutions," including expanded Orderly Departure migration directly from Vietnam, and "repatriation of those determined not to be bona fide refugees."[126]

A consortium of relief agencies in Thailand urged that the move to Site 2 not take place, stating:

> the camp is already desperately overcrowded and
> dangerous with unmanageable conditions . . . This
> danger is even more acute for the Vietnamese . . .
> surrounded by a vast population of Khmer with a
> historical animosity and the ever present danger
> of the Vietnamese (Communist) army.[127]

The voluntary agencies recommended that a "neutral site away from the war-torn border under UNHCR protection" be established. However, repeated appeals by the UNHCR and U.S. embassy to

---

[126] See "The Memorandum of Understanding on Arrangements of provision of Care and Shelter for Vietnamese Boat People in Thailand," dated April 20 1988.

[127] See voluntary agency "Message from Thailand Addressed to U.S. House Subcommittee on Asian and Pacific Affairs," February 23, 1988.

finance the reopening of camps at Sikhiu, Kamput or Kab Chhern were rejected by Thai officials.[128] By late May, close to 2,500 Vietnamese had been moved to Ban Thad.

During an October 1988 visit to Ban Thad, the Lawyers Committee found conditions in the camp comparable to the Khmer sections of Site 2. This contrasted with the impressions of Ban Thad by other western observers in June 1988. During the Lawyers Committee's October 4-5, 1988 visit to Ban Thad, the population was 3,460, but was expected to expand by at least 50 percent in November, when the "Land Vietnamese" from the Platform and Section 5 not accepted for resettlement were to be moved into Ban Thad.[129]

The UNHCR maintains a staff office in Ban Thad, where they are permitted a 24-hour access. However, due to limited staff, UN personnel generally spent an average of only one night per week during September and October in Ban Thad. Internal camp security is provided by Vietnamese camp leaders and an unarmed security team that maintains radio contact with the DPPU in case of a serious incident. The camp leader, Mr. Nguyen Huu Giao, a human rights lawyer from Vietnam, told the Committee in October 1988 that, following the departure of Task Force 80, serious problems in the camp involving Thai guards had ceased.

---

[128] See "Government Rejects U.S. Refugee Camp Request," Bangkok Post, February 3, 1988. Also, on May 2, 1988, a UNHCR representative told the Lawyers Committee that the agency "had proposed an alternative inland site such as Kamput," to Thai officials, stating that "Site 2 is too dangerous." Although UNCHR gave assurances that "there is no shortage of money or facilities," the Thai refused to consider the proposal.

[129] The majority of the Ban Thad population arrived in Thailand in early 1988 during the early stages of Thailand policy to deny asylum to most boat refugees. In August 1988 only 15 new arrivals entered the camp, and 134 in September, including land Vietnamese who walked across the nearby Cambodian border.

VI. UNITED STATES REFUGEE PROCESSING IN THAILAND

A. Background

There are a number of way for those fleeing Vietnam, Cambodia, and Laos to gain entry to the United States. The most common method has been admission as refugees under the Refugee Act of 1980. Refugee status is granted under Section 101(a)(42) of the U. S. Immigration and Nationality Act (the Act) to persons who have "a well-founded fear of persecution on account of race, religion, nationality, membership in a particular social group or political opinion."

Each fiscal year, the President with the approval of Congress sets numerical ceilings for the number of refugees to be admitted. Both the number of refugee openings worldwide and the number of these spaces set aside for southeast Asia have decreased each year since 1980. In 1980, the worldwide total was set at 231,700 with 169,200 spaces set aside for Southeast Asians. In 1988, the worldwide total was 94,000 with 53,000 Southeast Asian spaces. In percentage terms, the ceiling on Southeast Asian refugees has fluctuated between 56 and 76 percent of the total number of refugee admissions, the high coming in 1981 and the low coming in 1988. In accordance with the ceilings, the number of actual approvals of applications for refugee status also has generally declined, although there have been fluctuations due to changing events and conditions in Vietnam, Cambodia and Laos.

To aid in the processing of the large number of refugee applications, a group of qualifying categories has been developed by the U.S. Department of State and the Immigration and Naturalization Service (INS). These categories represent groups of people who are considered more likely to have a well-founded fear of persecution if returned to their home countries. The categories include ethnic Chinese from Vietnam or Cambodia, Buddhist monks, former U.S. employees, and Hmong from Laos. Despite the use of such aids, mere inclusion in a category does not assure a grant of refugee status. Furthermore, in the case of Cambodians, it is argued that many persons have been labelled, correctly or incorrectly, as members of the Khmer Rouge, and thereby have become ineligible for refugee status under Section 101(a) (42) of the Act for having participated in past persecution. In the case of Vietnamese and Laotians, disputes have arisen as to whether persons should be labelled as economic migrants instead of as refugees.

Refugees are also processed according to priorities developed by the State Department and the INS. Those with higher priorities are admitted first until the ceilings have been reached. The six priorities, in descending order, are: "exceptional cases" either of refugee in immediate danger of death or of compelling concern to the U.S.; former U. S. government employees; family reunification; other ties to the U.S.; additional family reunification (more distant family relations); and those with no ties to the U.S. but who are otherwise of national interest. Since the end of April 1982, the U. S. has not processed any refugees from Southeast Asia who fall within the Sixth priority, but there has been recent discussion about processing such individuals.

Although not a primary subject of this report, it should be noted that in addition to admission as refugees, persons fleeing Indochina can also gain entry thorough normal immigration channels. Immigrant visas are issued according to "preferences," with immediate relatives of U.S. citizens given top priority, followed by other relatives (of U.S. citizens and permanent residents) and those with special professional qualifications or skills in short supply. There is no limit on the number of immediate relatives of U.S. citizens who can be admitted. While many Indochinese refugees have not been in the U.S. for the minimum time required to qualify for citizenship, the large number who have become citizens may account for some of the drop in refugee ceilings, as persons come to the U. S. pursuant to immigrant visas instead of as refugees. The other immigrant visa preferences are limited.

A third method of gaining entry into the U. S. is "humanitarian parole." Humanitarian parole is granted at the discretion of the Attorney General, and its use has been limited since the institution of general refugee admissions under the Act. Parole admissions are not included in the refugee ceilings. Unlike the trend shown by the refugee ceilings and approval figures, the use of humanitarian parole has increased since 1980. There is a separate program for humanitarian parole of persons in the camps along the Thai-Cambodian border.

Finally, for people leaving Vietnam, there is a special program in place called the Orderly Departure program (ODP). The ODP was agreed to by Vietnam at the Geneva Conference in 1979, and is managed by the Office of the United Nations High Commissioner for Refugees. About 60,000 individual have come to the U. S. under this program since its inception. The Vietnamese government grants exit visas to those whom it is willing to allow to leave, and those persons are interviewed by the UNHCR and resettled abroad if they qualify.

The U.S. has had a particular interest in the ODP since 1984 when the President called for admission for Amerasians and one for political prisoners. These aspects of the ODP have been less successful than the initial family reunification program because they receive less support from the Vietnamese government.

On January 1, 1986, Vietnam suspended ODP interviews when the number of persons being resettled had fallen far behind the number who had been interviewed. This backlog had been cleared up and interviews were resumed following talks between the U.S. and Vietnam on July 13 and 14, 1987. During 1988, ODP departures have increased, primarily for Amerasians and in family reunification cases; however, few political prisoners have been able to leave Vietnam to date.

As the ODP requires the cooperation of the Vietnamese government to facilitate interviewing and processing, the other programs -- refugee admissions, immigrant visas and humanitarian parole -- require the cooperation of the country of first asylum. The thousands fleeing Vietnam, Cambodia, and Laos have required temporary refuge so as to gain access to the refugee processing procedures of the U.S. and other resettlement countries. The role of the country of first asylum has fallen generally to the other Southeast Asian countries, and particularly to Thailand. Hong Kong, Malaysia, Indonesia and a number of other countries have received Indochinese refugees, but Thailand has received far more. The extent of the Indochinese refugee crisis has placed a heavy burden on the first asylum countries, requiring many resources and much compassion from the countries themselves as well as close international cooperation.

The examples of the problem involving the countries of first asylum are most clear in the case of Thailand. Thailand has long accepted asylum seekers from its Southeast Asian neighbors. Its policy, though, is to act only as a country of first asylum, and not as a place of permanent resettlement. Because of this historical position, and of its geographical placement in the region, many of the Vietnamese, Cambodians, and Laotians fled their homelands for Thailand. When the flow of refugees reached its peak in 1979-80, Thailand found its resources overwhelmed by the large numbers. The Thai government began to turn away boats filled with Vietnamese and to push some of the arriving Cambodians and land Vietnamese back over the Thai-Cambodian border. It was only after quick international action in 1979, both by states at the Geneva Conference and by international organizations, that Thailand was willing to allow camps to be opened from which the refugees could be processed.

97

The motives behind the Thai decision illustrate some of the peculiar characteristics of the Southeast Asian situation in 1988. Once again, the Thai government was willing to give only temporary asylum after receiving assurances that the subjects would be resettled elsewhere. As the willingness of the resettlement countries to accept more Indochinese has waned, so too has the resolve of the Thai government to offer first asylum. One of the largest of the camps under UNHCR auspices, Khao I Dang, was closed by the Thai government on December 31, 1986. The government has stated that it will return the approximately 14,500 Cambodians (most of whom previously have been rejected for resettlement) to the Cambodian border. Although the government has not yet carried out this plan, except for illegal residents of Khao I Dang, a solution has not been found to the problem. The U.S. has recently received Thai permission to interview the 7,000 "ration cardholders" in the Khao I Dang Annex.

Similarly, particularly in the case of Cambodians and Laotians, the Thai government has been unwilling to allow more refugees into UNHCR-administered camps or to allow them to be interviewed for third country resettlement. This policy is in part due to the desire to discourage further flows into Thailand, but it also represents the political structure of the region. The Thai government opposes the Communist regimes in Cambodia and Laos, particularly the Vietnamese-installed Heng Samrin government of Cambodia. Hence, it is willing to allow guerrilla groups to form camps along the border, providing both a place for the guerrillas to rest and regroup and a buffer of Cambodians between Thailand and the Vietnamese army in Cambodia.

Repatriation of some individuals to the country from which they came is often mentioned as a partial solution to these problems. In the case of the Vietnamese, in the past repatriation has been unlikely because of distance and the antagonism of the Vietnamese government. Recently, however, Vietnam has indicated that it is willing to take back those who volunteer to return. The Thai government has also publicly expressed an interest in the eventual repatriation of all Vietnamese declared "illegal aliens."

The Cambodian government has in the past been antagonistic to repatriation, especially considering the number of opposition forces in the border camps. However, there has been some support for repatriation from the Heng Samrin regime more recently and the Thai government assumes that repatriation will eventually be an option.

The Laotian government has been more amenable to repatriation, and in 1985 entered into an agreement to take back Laotians who are determined to be without a refugee claim when screened at the Thai-Laotian border. The agreement, though, has not been honored, although voluntary repatriation to Laos has been allowed.

B. Description of The Process

The U.S. refugee process in Thailand involves many actors. The initial screening for Vietnamese, Khmer, and Laotians is conducted by members of the Joint Voluntary Agency (JVA), an arm of the International Rescue Committee which is under contract with the U.S. State Department. JVA caseworkers interview those who are applying for admission to the U.S. as refugees, in order to find out basic biographical information and to identify which persons may have sympathetic cases for resettlement. JVA officials conduct the basic background work on a case so that it is ready for presentation to the INS, and attempt to identify difficult cases which require further study. A JVA caseworker also completes preliminary forms giving biographic details and family history trees, does initial processing/classification of a case and grouping together of related family members into one case file, and makes sure that all proper documentation, both official forms as well as informal correspondence, is in a case file.

If questions arise, or in certain categories of cases, an Ethnic Affairs Officer (EAO) employed by the State Department will be consulted. For example, an individual claiming that he was a military officer in South Vietnam, or that he has worked with the U.S. government, will be referred to an EAO who will attempt to verify that claim. Although in theory the EAO's are the "experts" to check difficult cases, in reality they have a variety of backgrounds, and some are merely former JVA caseworkers.

The EAO can conduct a further interview of the applicant. The EAO meets everyone included in the same case, and then interviews them separately. Discrepancies with JVA notes, and discrepancies between family members, raise credibility issues which the EAO attempts to reconcile. As of October 1988, Congress and the State Department were considering eliminating EAO's from the processing system.

Formal INS processing occurs after these initial reviews, and after the file is checked to confirm that it contains the necessary

99

information. Once again, the applicant is interviewed, this time by an INS officer, with the benefit of any prior information from JVA caseworkers and/or an EAO. The interview is conducted by an INS officer working with an interpreter, and according to the Worldwide guidelines for overseas Refugee Processing is to be conducted under oath. This is an informal process, and there is no right to an attorney or other representation. If the individual has any documentation, such as re-education camp certificates or military identification, he can present it to the INS officer, just as it could be presented to the JVA caseworker. The interviews occur in buildings at the border camps themselves, and may take about an hour. Following the interview, but not immediately thereafter, the individual is notified as to whether he has been accepted or rejected for resettlement. Under the Act, the burden of proof rests on the applicant to establish refugee status.

Under recently promulgated confidential guidelines, the INS can inform a rejected individual of documents that are needed to support the claim, but not of the reasons for denial, or the evidence needed to overcome an adverse ruling. Denied applicants generally receive a form response. Access to INS files can be obtained only though an Freedom of Information Act request. The INS states that the confidentiality rules exist because it is concerned about the retailoring of further applications, and the burden that would be placed on INS in responding to a plethora of inquires concerning its reason for denials. Nevertheless, these confidentiality rules make the procedures, and the evidence needed to make a satisfactory presentation to the INS, more mysterious and difficult.

According to the Guidelines, cases rejected by the INS are sent to a supervisory officer for a review within ten days. If the denial is upheld, then the case is sent to the "officer-in-charge (if other than the first line supervisor)" for a decision within ten days. In most cases, this ends any right to review. If however, the applicant falls into one of the approved categories of groups targeted for persecution in a country, as specified in the Guidelines, then the case is transmitted to the INS District Director in Bangkok for a decision within ten days. A denial of one of these cases by the District Director results in further review by the INS office of Refugee, Asylum, and Parole in Washington, D.C. All of these procedures, however, while noted in the Guidelines, have little practical effect on decisions, and very few decisions are reversed. Officials reviewing the files have only a paper record from the interviews before them, and so are hesitant to reverse prior decisions.

In addition, the INS has indicated that rejected cases may be re-presented if new evidence arises, such as previously unpresented documentation to support claims. This is not a systematic procedure, but rather occurs on an ad hoc basis. As cases become known and representation seems desirable, an additional INS interview, similar to that conducted previously, may be scheduled.

For those rejected, immigrant visas or humanitarian parole, may still be an option. Immigrant visas are based upon status in certain preference categories. Access the humanitarian parole, is, by contrast, discretionary under authority of the Attorney General and rarely granted. After requests for parole come to the attention of INS officials, cases are prepared by JVA caseworkers, with ultimate decisions made by the INS. Requests for parole can be submitted by almost any person interested in being a sponsor, including a relative, member of Congress, or private organization. The requests must contain specific information, including the individual's name, place and date of birth, identification numbers, and camp where he or she is located. In addition, the sponsor must submit information about its relationship to the individual, how it will meet basic needs of the person (e.g., food, clothing), an affidavit of support, and a statement of why parole is appropriate. The determinations are discretionary and are made by the INS District Director in Bangkok. There are no guidelines for deciding when such parole is proper.

C. Problems with the Processing System

The system of refugee processing described above suffers from a number of defects. First, staffing and training of personnel to engage in the processing has been inadequate. Second, there has been a lack of adequate guidelines and country conditions information for those persons involved in processing. Third, the review process itself does not contain adequate guarantees of fairness, and should at least require INS officers to issue written statements of findings and reasons supporting a determination. Finally, there has been a lack of any effective mechanism for appeal and review of denied cases.

1. Staffing and Training

There appears to be a consensus that the current personnel involved in processing (in particular the INS officers) are, on the whole, a more cohesive unit and more competent than in preceding years. This statement, however, betrays an understanding of prior problems, and of the fact that the process itself has become overly dependent on the personalities involved and on the competence of the individuals currently engaged in the processing. Instead, there should be adequate recruitment, training, and quality control such that refugee determinations will be fair and accurate irrespective of the individuals sent to do the job. This can be achieved through a variety of means.

Hiring and Recruitment. First, the INS processing system is subject to the severe restrictions imposed by having a very limited staff to engage in reviews. As of October 1988, there were eight INS officers stationed in Thailand. Additional officers, however, are necessary to engage in an adequate review of the large number of persons seeking refugee status. This is especially true in light of the recent expansion of ODP. Every month, INS sends three officers to Vietnam for periods ranging from one to two weeks in order to conduct ODP interviews. In addition, generally there are only four INS officers in the field at any given time, while one or two officers remain in Bangkok, doing central office work. Obviously, there are not enough people to perform all these functions.

Although individual INS officers may have been in the foreign service, the persons involved in processing generally have no background in Southeast Asian affairs. Fluency in Thai gives bonus points toward obtaining an INS position in Thailand, however such knowledge is not required, nor is fluency in other Indochinese languages a requirement. Similarly, no such requirements of fluency or experience apply to JVA caseworkers or to EAO's. As a result, with the exception of one EAO, there is apparently no one involved in processing who has any language training in Khmer or Laotian. Traditionally, even the "experts", the EAO's have often been drawn merely from person who are former JVA caseworkers, without any other substantive political knowledge of conditions in the area. However, in October 1988, a State Department official indicated that the EAO staff included a number of EAO's who had lived in Vietnam or Cambodia. INS officials have requested that officers assigned to Thailand be experienced in the area, and in general expressed concern that even if funds were available for hiring there would not be suitable individuals available for the position.

To meet the need for INS personnel, assignment of individuals to INS processing positions has often been for only a temporary period, as Temporary Duty Officers ("TDY"). Assignment is usually for a 60-day period (or at most 90 days). This merely exacerbates the problem. TDY's do not have prior experience, and do not have the opportunity to develop practical experience, and do not have the opportunity to develop practical experience in processing so that they become more proficient over a period of time. The inexperience of these individuals, combined with their temporary assignment, further heightens the risk of inconsistent decisions and of incorrect decisions, and at least one official classified the systemic use of TDY's as "inherently bad."

Recently, for example, use of TDY'S resulted in the rejection of a large group of Lowland Laotians located at the Na Pho detention camp. The cases of 200 such individuals, rejected by TDY's, were re-reviewed by INS officers in January 1988. Discussions with each individual lasted for about one hour or more. When the review was completed, approximately 50 percent of the previous rejections had been overturned. In other words, the INS interviewers decided that there had been a 50 percent error rate in the prior determinations by TDY's of ineligibility for resettlement. The INS team leader for the reinterviews noted that often the TDY's had not gone deeply enough into a person's background, including evidence of family ties and of persecution. In other cases, individuals presented documents they had not presented initially, possibly, the team leader speculated, because they had been frightened at the initial interview.

Training. Similarly, for those individuals engaged in INS processing there must be background training in order to ensure that the decision-making process is reliable and based in fact and law. In the past, INS officers have received no training prior to undertaking interviews. The only training that exists has been that new officers are informally taken around to be introduced the the current JVA caseworkers and EAOP's. Following this, the new people begin engaging in interviews. Although we were told by the District Director that INS team leaders review the work product of new officers more closely than that of experienced officers, there has, to date, been no formal review or oversight process.

In January 1988, INS officials stated that they intended to initiate a formal training program. However, nine months later, such a program has not been established. It would appear that INS's "plans" for a training program were limited to a single three-day training session for a group of TDY's in March 1988. In fact, in October 1988, officials indicated that they did not intend to establish a formal, ongoing training program, stating that such a program would be impractical because few officers started their assignment at the same time.

Nonetheless, training programs can be designed to accommodate INS's hiring practices. For example, written and videotaped materials might be used. Any adequate training must encompass several elements. There must, of course, be training about the legal standards and guidelines to be applied in deciding if refugee status is warranted. This also must include training on political conditions in the relevant countries in order to determine what individuals are validly fleeing persecution.

In addition, however, such training should also include language and/or cultural training. Numerous individuals described to us cultural differences which, if not known to an interviewer, might color his or her perception of a person's credibility. For example, it was noted that many Indochinese retain neutral, or even pleasant, affect even when describing events of great tragedy. Thus, the death of relatives may be described without apparent grief, or even perhaps interspersed with periodic laughter. This is apparently a cultural difference from American society, in that many Khmer feel it is improper to show their grief. Nevertheless, an American INS official, unfamiliar with such behavior, may feel that the interviewee is being deceitful in describing past events.

The training program also should include organizations such as UNHCR and other international relief agencies and non-governmental organizations. The involvement of such groups would prove useful in order to explain their role and to help provide general background on those individuals in the camps. UNHCR, at least, plays a particularly important role, since for each individual and each case they prepare a computer printout containing basic biographic and family information.

Quality Control. Finally, quality control checks are necessary in order to ensure the determinations are being made consistently between different examiners. In January 1988, the District of the INS Bangkok office indicated that, at that time, a tracking system was being initiated in order to keep track of individual officers and their approval and denial rates for persons they interview. However, in October 1988, the District Director stated that, although weekly monitoring of approval and denial rates was conducted, the approval and denial rates of individual officers were not monitored. INS acknowledged however, that they were aware of complaints regarding inconsistencies in determinations.

To address such complaints and ensure a modicum of fairness, a tracking system is necessary to determine whether certain examiners are exhibiting biases, either generally or for certain classes of individuals. On a most elementary level, if rejection rates vary greatly between interviewers, then there should be a review of the individual cases and discussion of why evaluations differ. Each INS officer should be using the same standards, and acceptance as a refugee should not be dependent on who conducts the interview.

Quality control should also include oversight to be sure that interview procedures are adequate and that questioning of the applicant has been thorough and fair. One apparently Amerasian boy rejected by the INS, for example, complained that his INS interview lasted for only fifteen minutes.

Finally, even for those experienced in interviewing, periodic "continuing education" would be desirable. This could serve to provide updates as to recent legal or country-specific developments, and to share ideas and problems regarding the decision process.

2. Legal Guidelines and Country Condition Information

The best training and quality control will, of course, be ineffective if incorrect legal standards are applied or if out-of-date country information is utilized. In this regard, the latest information provided to INS officers is the criteria found in the 1983 Worldwide Guidelines, criteria which are now obsolete in may respects. Similarly, the most recent country conditions reports for Laos, Cambodia, and Vietnam also date from 1983. Updated and accurate information is needed.

Cardoza-Fonseca For example, the 1983 Guidelines are inconsistent in their designation of the appropriate standard of proof by which adjudicators are to assess refugee claims -- the "well-founded fear" of persecution criterion found applicable by the Supreme Court in its March 1987 *Cardoza-Fonseca* case.[130] Since the Guidelines were written in 1983, the legal standard cited, including references to whether persecution is "realistically likely", is now obsolete. Not only should the proper standard be clearly and consistently reflected in the Guidelines, but it should also be used to review any cases denied under more stringent standards which were at times used prior to the *Cardoza-Fonseca* decision.

Guidelines for Evaluating Claims. The Worldwide Guidelines are deficient for other reasons as well. The Guidelines note several general categories of individuals coming from Vietnam, Cambodia, or

---

[130] *INS v. Cardoza-Fonseca*, _____U./S._____, 107, S. Ct. 1207 (1987).

105

Laos, who, under the Refugee Act of 1980, are "likely targets" of persecution. These categories include, for example, former government officials, former military, persons employed by Western institutions, educated in the West, or who have worked in refugee programs, and persons put in re-education camps or imprisoned. The categories, while useful, are not necessarily definitive in establishing a refugee claim. Indeed, at least several dozen persons interviewed claimed to have been former military, and/or to have been in re-education camps, one of the categories under the Guidelines. Nevertheless, these individuals were rejected by the INS. At Site 2 former Vietnamese military officers presented a listing of former South Vietnamese officers at the camp, including the status of their applications to resettle in the U.S. Numerous persons are noted on the list as having been rejected by the INS.

Thus the categories standing alone appear to have minimal effect. This stems in part from the fact that the Guidelines offer little insight into two difficult areas on which many or most rejections are based, namely that a person has either participated in persecution or is of dubious credibility. Detailed guidelines are necessary in these areas.

First, the current guidelines fail to provide criteria by which an adjudicator is to determine whether a refugee is unworthy of protection by virtue of having persecuted others. In particular, many individuals on the Cambodian border are suspected of having participated in persecution committed by the Khmer Rouge. Under U.S. law, "[t]he term 'refugee' does not include any person who has ordered, incited, assisted or otherwise participated in the persecution of any person on account of race, religion, nationality, membership in a particular social group, or political opinion."[131] Denials on this ground have affected thousands of Cambodians currently held at Khao I Dang. Nevertheless, there has been no practical guidance on what level of activity a person must have engaged in order to be considered a "persecutor", or how to weigh the relevant evidence. The result is that interpretations by EAO's and/or by individual INS officers can be inconsistent, varying greatly.

In an attempt to establish clear guidelines for determining when an individual should be ineligible for resettlement due to persecution of others, the Lawyers Committee has previously proposed the following:

---

[131] 8 U.S.C. Section 101(a) (42)(A)

-- The "persecution of others" exception is a narrow and limited exception to the definition of a "refugee"; any interpretation of this exclusionary provision must be restrictive in light of the serious consequences of a determination denying protection to an individual who, by definition, nevertheless has a well-founded fear of persecution.

-- The INS officers should go forward with proof on the persecutor issue in order to give an applicant a reasonable opportunity to explain any derogatory information. The applicant need submit rebuttal evidence only upon the INS officer being satisfied that there is substantial proof that the applicant participated in the persecution of others.

-- A decision to deny an applicant refugee status should be based on reliable and credible evidence, such as authenticated written documents credible, detained, non-hearsay accounts made by individuals with personal knowledge, or reliable and credible intelligence reports furnished by the U.S. Government. General temporal or geographical evidence is not reliable or conclusive proof justifying a decision to deny refugee status.

-- Where proof of participation in persecution is based upon circumstantial evidence, the applicant should be denied refugee status only if the inferences exclude to a moral certainty every reasonable hypothesis of innocence.

-- Refugee status should be denied based only on active and personal participation in the persecution of others or active and effective membership in an organization which is devoted to the persecution of others.

-- Mere membership in an organization which is involved in the persecution of others should be an insufficient basis to conclude that an applicant participated in the persecution of others.

-- Participation in acts of persecution under duress does not justify the denial of refugee status; duress should be a sufficient and complete defense to the charge of persecution of others.

-- In resolving factual disputes and assessing the available evidence, an applicant for refugee status should be given the benefit of the doubt.

In general, it is important that uniform guidelines be established, so that the process is fair. Absent such guidance, inconsistencies cannot be avoided.

There is also inadequate guidance as to how to make determinations in a second important area, namely creditability. Evidentiary considerations similar to those noted for the "persecution of others" exception should be considered in this area as well. Thus, a decision to deny an applicant refugee status should be based on reliable and credible evidence, and not on general temporal or geographic evidence. Where proof is based upon circumstantial evidence, the applicant should be denied refugee status only if the inferences exclude every reasonable hypothesis of innocence. Finally, in resolving factual disputes and assessing the available evidence, an applicant for refugee status should be given the benefit of the doubt. Specific guidance as to what constitutes an "economic migrant" should also be drafted and implemented, including guidance as to types of economics hardship that may be a result of persecution.

Country Condition Information. Just as the legal guideline must be complete, so too factual information on conditions in Laos, Cambodia, and Vietnam must be as complete as possible. Unfortunately, the country condition reports on which INS officers rely date from 1983, and they therefore require revision. INS officers did, however, indicate that they had some updated reports on certain countries, distinct from country condition reports compiled by the State Department.

Up-to-date information is crucial to proper evaluation of claims of individuals coming to Thailand, including evaluation of the credibility of stories proferred to INS officers. This is particularly true since determinations have been made in whole or in part based on facts such as an individual's presence in a particular time, e.g., if the person was present in a location, he is thought to have possibly been a Khmer Rouge sympathizer.

Thus, a report of the Department of State and Justice noted that JVA caseworkers look to at least two important facts to determine whether an EAO review is necessary regarding possible Khmer Rouge affiliation: (1) is the person in, or from, a border camp controlled by the Khmer Rouge, (2) is the person a "base person", i.e., a member of the poor peasants who were the heart of Khmer Rouge support. In addition, the report noted that there are five basic areas of inquiry made by an EAO to determine whether an individual has Khmer Rouge ties:

1. Where was the person born and where was he or she living when the Khmer Rouge arrived?

2. What occurred when the Khmer Rouge arrived?

3. Where was the person moved by the Khmer Rouge?

4. What was the person's employment while the Khmer Rouge was in power?

5. What occurred when the Vietnamese arrived?

None of these generalizations are necessarily accurate, and none of the inquiries result in solid grounds for determining Khmer Rouge affiliation, without accurate and current country information.

INS officials expressed the desire for more recent country condition material, but such material has not been provided. In addition, it was suggested that intelligence information should be provided in the background information, including relevant names and dates in order to thoroughly check information from those in the camps regarding army services or presence in re-education camps. Without this current information, evaluations must be based upon information which can be out of date, in particular for person who have fled to Thailand since 1983.

Background material is informally made available to the INS interviewers though various cables and handbooks, such as the JVA handbook. This material includes specific information in areas such as the identification of government units, army division, locations of re-education camps, chronologies of political developments, etc., which is important information in order to check the credibility of the individuals in the camps. Nevertheless, provision of such material is sporadic, and the material is not kept up to date. INS officials further informed us that they have no readily available library of materials on country conditions in Cambodia, Laos, or Vietnam, and that there is no continuing education to familiarize persons with current academic literature in this area.

One INS officer also suggested that opportunities to travel to a country such as Vietnam would be useful for INS officers, in order to gather country condition information. It was admitted, however, that under current political conditions any travel to that country is tightly regulated, so that it would be difficult to gather meaningful data for the purpose of making evaluations of refugee claims.

Examples. Although precise reasons for INS denials cannot always be determined, due to confidentiality rules, a number of individual cases suggest that they may have been rejected by the INS based on a combination of improper criteria and/or generalizations about country conditions which are unfounded in fact. The most common problem is probably the use of generalized "stereotypes" about country conditions, e.g., persons engaged in a certain activity or from a certain activity or from a certain area are thought to have helped the Khmer Rouge. Such stereotypes place an onerous evidentiary burden on the applicant, and absent updated, reliable country condition material such blanket generalizations are unfounded in fact. For example, it has been stated that schoolteachers are usually rejected by the INS based on presumption that teachers worked with, and are sympathetic to, the current government and therefore do not fear persecution. It seems unlikely, however, that all teachers are cooperating with the government, no matter how innocent the subject that they teach. Criteria should be established so that such generalizations cannot be relied upon to reject an otherwise meritorious case.

Another stereotype that has been criticized is that persons working for the Laotian government after 1975 cannot have a valid persecution claim. In reality, however, numerous individuals stated that they only worked for the Laotian government under duress, and often did menial work not commensurate with their title. Two individuals at Na Pho, for example, had sympathetic cases, but said that the INS had raised questions due to their having been forced to work for the Laotian government after 1975. Veopradith Khoukham, who has a brother and sister in Minnesota, has two Ph'd's from the University of Bordeaux in France. He was put in re-education camp for approximately three years, and was jailed on political activity charges for over a year. His difficulty is that he says he was forced to work for the Laotian government after 1975 in various official titles. His actual work, however, was allegedly merely menial labor, including feeding animals and cutting wood at a chicken farm.

Similarly, Sitthivong Phengsavanh, who received an M.A. in Paris and a law degree in Laos, was deputy director of the Finance Ministry in Laos prior to the Pathet Lao government. His wife and

110

two children live in Illinois. He, as well as his three brothers (before 1975 two of them were directors in government ministries and one was a lieutenant colonel in the army) and his father-in -law, were all placed in re-education camps. Later, he was forced to work in the Finance Ministry, and allegedly as a result of that activity has been rejected by the INS. This despite the fact that after his escape to Thailand he was also allegedly engaged in intelligence work for the U.S. government for several years.

These cases illustrate the need for reliable criteria and accurate country condition information in order to evaluate these generalized grounds for denial. Such "stereotypes" should not be used to deny an individual refugee status absent such safeguards.

3. Fairness of the Interview Process

The refugee interview process itself is unfair. This section explores the interview process, and in particular the key role of credibility determinations in resolving individual cases.

Credibility Determinations. Generally, individuals are rejected by the INS either because they do not meet refugee criteria or because their stories are deemed not credible. These two areas tend, in practice, to overlap. Thus, the two reasons cited most often as the grounds for rejection of refugee claims can both be highly dependent on assessments of individual credibility: (1) in the case of Cambodians, many individuals are rejected due to a suspicion that they participated in persecution conducted by the Khmer Rouge, and (2) in the case of Vietnamese and Laotians, many individuals are rejected due to a suspicion that they are economic migrants, rather than persons fleeing from persecution

In both these cases, clear guidelines and country condition information are necessary, as discussed above, but there must also be a determination of whether the story presented, and the fear of persecution, is credible. Often, if not in most cases, the denial of refugee status is therefore based on a combination of one of the above factors combined with credibility issues. The importance of the determination of an individual's credibility at an interview is in fact noted in the Guidelines: "[t]estimony by the applicant is frequently all that is available, and if that testimony is credible, it is sufficient to establish a claim to refugee status."

Despite their importance, adverse determinations on credibility issues are virtually impossible for applicants to overcome or rebut, based largely on the fact that, under applicable confidentiality guidelines, INS officers cannot give applicants specific findings or statements of reasons for their decision denying refugee status. In this way an INS officer can merely rely on a general impression of lack of facts. By contrast, if more formal findings were required to be given to applicants, then review of credibility determinations would be possible, and effective oversight of individual decisions could occur. If doubts about credibility could be rebutted or could be shown to have resulted from a translation error, then reversal of an adverse decision could be more readily accomplished. Similarly, more formal findings would also strengthen the basis for denial of claims when denial is appropriate, by pointing to concrete difficulties with an individual's case.

Specific problems with making determinations in the interviews, and in determining credibility, are discussed in more detail below. Many of the problems could be alleviated both through the use of specific findings and reasons, and also through greater awareness and training of interviewers.

Translators and Cultural Differences. Problems with translators can result in apparent inconsistencies in an individual's story. Translators are generally individuals in the camps who have been approved for resettlement; however, as a general policy the interpreters do not live in the camps. Although an attempt is made to obtain competent translators, the process is imperfect.

The problem is that if difficulties in translation or mistranslation occur, then through no fault of the individual the INS interviewer may come to doubt an individual's credibility, and may deny the refugee application. At least one commentator has in the past noted this problem with regard to the Khmer camps and cited an example of different translators disagreeing over an interpretation.[132] This problem is difficult to correct, but training in how to deal with translators, as well as opportunities for an effective appeal after a written statement of findings and reasons would help mitigate this problem.

The guidelines give a page of general advice on dealing with translators, which should be expanded upon through training and oversight. For example, the Guidelines suggest that, to aid translation, questions should be "straight-forward and generally short"

---

[132] S. Golub, *Flaws in the Interpretation of INA Section 101(a) (42) and in the Denial of Refugee Status to Cambodians in Thailand*, 70 Georgetown Immigration Law Journal, 1, 30 (1985).

and that slang and technical terms should be avoided. This advice seems logical, but is undoubtedly easier to read than to practice.

As discussed previously, there may also be cross-cultural difficulties which impede effective translation and which could be discussed during training of new INS officers. To the extent such cultural differences prevent an accurate determination of a case, INS officers should be able to recognize these differences.

Lack of Documents. Many individuals who were former military or government officials may have destroyed personal records and identification in an attempt to hide their identify from the Khmer Rouge or Pathet Lao. The importance of having documents to corroborate claims must therefore be kept in its proper perspective, and should not be a prerequisite for relief. Ironically, a person's attempt to escape persecution by destroying documents can also make their claim of refugee status more difficult. Song Huynh, for example, was arrested and imprisoned in Vhetman, and says that his family destroyed documents in 1975 for fear of persecution. His family was rejected by the INS however, because they were told they needed documents to prove that their father was a hamlet chief in Vietnam. Nguyen Dang Giam states that he is a former Vietnamese army officer who was put in re-education for two years; he was told he was rejected by the INS for lack of a photo from his army days.

While INS officials state that they do not rely heavily on documents and that they try to give applicants the benefit of the doubt, statements made by INS officials indicate otherwise. For example, according to the INS District Director in Bangkok, unaccompanied minors are asked to obtain documents to establish that a parent served in the Vietnamese army. The District Director stated that there is mail service between Thailand and Vietnam and that INS cannot assume that everyone is telling the truth.

Fabricated Stories. Another problem with the interview process can occur when individuals at the camps are told that certain stories will result in rejection (or acceptance) by the INS. As a result individuals may fabricate what they are told is a "good story", in order to attempt to impress INS officers. This of course tends to backfire, because inconsistencies are found in the story, either during the course of an interview or during the course of comparison of that interview to other interviews of the applicant or his or her family. Once inconsistencies are found the individual is in a difficult dilemma, even if he or she wishes to tell the true story, and is encouraged to do so by the INS. If the person decides to change his or her story and tell the truth, then the number of inconsistent stories increases; if the person continues to lie then the already existing inconsistencies remain.

It is impossible to tell how often this problem occurs, but it was mentioned often, including by an INS team leader and by UNHCR officials who stated that they had warned those in the camps to avoid this practice. Indeed, the presence of camp gossip regarding "good stories" may be seen by the fact that several people made statements during interviews regarding the "godlessness and oppression of Communism", often using these words in a manner which suggested they were merely a stock phrase.

A compelling example of a person allegedly harmed by use of a fabricated story is May Chan La, a man at Na Pho with his wife and even children. Three other children of his are currently living in Connecticut. May Chan La produced copies of numerous documents, including certificates of training from American University, Northwest University, and the Agency for International development, and in fact he serves as the camp librarian at Na Pho. He was a teacher in Laos, and a soldier from 1953 to 1956. From 1976 to 1984, he was placed in a re-education camp. Nevertheless, he says that people in the camp told him that the INS would never believe that he had been in a re-education camp for eight years. As a result, he lied and said that he had been working in a rice field during that time. The INS apparently did not find this story credible and therefore rejected his application for resettlement, despite a compelling case for a well-founded fear of persecution.

Individuals who fabricate stories often have no need to do so. Lor Xeng is Hmong currently at Phanat Nikhom. He fled Laos because his father was in the military prior to 1975. After staying in a camp for three years, he got married and illegally left the camp in 1978. (although he stayed in Thailand). In 1984, he was discovered by Thai authorities and returned to a camp. When the INS interviewed him he was concerned that he would be rejected if he admitted having illegally left the camp; instead he therefore told the INS that returned to Laos from 1978 to 1984. By fabricating this story, however, he raised doubts as to whether he would be persecuted if returned to Laos, and he was rejected by the INS.

At times, an individual may fabricate a story, but then also note in an offhand manner a fact which would show persecution. Thus, the interview process must be probing, and carefully conducted. Khamsourin Amphone, a man at Na Pho who has a brother and sister in California, is a case in point. His story is confused, and it is difficult to know what to believe since he says he was in prison, but says he was afraid to tell this to the INS. At the close of an interview, with him however, he mentioned that he was currently helping the resistance fighters who are fighting the current Laotian government. Although it may be debated whether active resistance members should be allowed to resettle in the U.S., these facts were among the best evidence that could be presented by him to support his refugee claim.

In addition to applicants fabricating stories about their own lives, another problem is that at times persons in the camp fabricate stories about others in the camp, in an attempt to hurt those other persons. This may be done out of spite or due to a dispute between families. Thus, even if an individual's story is consistent and shows likely persecution, issues can arise. In cases such as these, where a credible story exists, guidelines are necessary. The INS should only reject the individual based on credible contrary evidence from an extrinsic source; the inferences drawn should be resolved in favor of the applicant. A written decision would further allow review of whether the credibility decision appears proper.

An example of the need to give the benefit of the doubt to refugees in assessing credibility is provided by Mohamach, a Vietnamese boy in Site 2, who looks Western, and says that he is half-American. His adopted mother was jailed three times because of his father's alleged work with the CIA. He was allegedly rejected by the INS due to the fact that he could not prove he was half-American, as opposed to half-European, and due to the fact that someone not in his family told the INS that his brother is currently a soldier in Cambodia (which, if true, would tend to discount any fear of his being persecuted in Cambodia). He insists that his brother is not a soldier, and does not know who has spread this rumor. Nevertheless, he has no concrete way to rebut it since his brother is in Cambodia, and therefore he remains denied.

Failures of Recollection. Other cases are denied due to the failure of an individual to list a family member on a "family tree", or to accurately recall information about a relative. Immigration officials routinely gather information from those in the camps to accumulate family trees. Minor discrepancies can have severe consequences, despite the fact that families can be quite large and therefore the presence of minor errors would seem excusable. In particular, for each case a list of family members is gathered by JVA caseworkers, and information supplied is compared both between applicants in the same case, and also with information gathered from other cases. Indeed, the JVA even has a form letter to be sent to relatives who came to the U.S. from Thailand, in order to resolve contradictory information in those cases where an individual in the camps contradicts evidence which had previously been obtained from the relative.

In this area in particular, minor discrepancies should not serve as the basis for denials of refugee status. Written findings and reasons by the INS should be required so that an independent judgment can be made as to whether discrepancies are material, and so that unwarranted discrepancies can be corrected. It must be remembered that the ultimate question is whether there is a well-founded fear of persecution; this is not a memory test.

If an individual forgets to note a relative, two problems may arise. First, the applicant may be deemed not credible, and may therefore be rejected by the INS. Pasao Thao, a 72 year-old Laotian now at Phanat Nikhom, has 11 children, three of whom are living in Minnesota. Information received on this man indicates that problems arose when he failed to recall the name of one of his children, even though he has a strong claim for refugee status based on his statements that from 1975 to 1978 he and his family went into hiding and helped the resistance forces. His failure to recollect one name seems a minor omission. Indeed, this man may have been forgetful due to his age. (After his interview with the Lawyers Committee he walked away without his UNHCR identification material.)

Other failures of recollection can relate to details of a family member's life. Dai Lien Chau states that she came from Vietnam, where her husband is in prison. She was rejected by the INS allegedly due to her failure to answer questions about her husband's military service, even though her husband was only a soldier prior to their marriage.

Alternatively, other family members who tell stories inconsistent with the family tree mentioned by a particular individual may find themselves rejected. Sisombath Lucky's parents live in the U.S. His father allegedly worked form the secret police in Laos, and later fled to Thailand and applied for resettlement. His mother was able to flee to Thailand at a later date. When she and her husband were accepted by the INS for resettlement, she decided they had best accept that offer. Of course, they remained concerned about Lucky and their other children who remained in Laos. Soon the children were able to escape to Thailand on their own. The children, however, were later rejected by the INS due to confusion over the family tree. This confusion appears to involve a combination of a mistranscription of ages (a younger child was listed by the INS as having an earlier birthdate), and inconsistencies in listing the names of deceased children. Apparently, some family members listed the deceased children on their family tree but some did not, and the inconsistency led the INS to raise issues of credibility. This regardless of the evidence of a well-found fear of persecution, and regardless of the resultant separation of the family.

Dang Xuan Hong is another example. He has three years of medical school training, worked in the Cambodian government, and has two aunts and an uncle in the U.S. Nevertheless he was rejected by the INS, allegedly due to doubts regarding his relation to his brother.

As a result of these types of problems, as well as the general credibility concerns noted above, individuals at the camps become paranoid about whether they should tell the INS the identical information that they told JVA caseworkers and EAO's. On several occasions, people interviewed returned after the interview to indicate that they had not told certain information to the INS and that as a result they would be very upset if it was revealed at this time, thus casting doubt on their prior credibility. One man in Site 2 therefore asked that we not reveal the fact that the Vietnamese government in Cambodia had seized all of his family's property.

4. Appeal and Review

These problems are exacerbated by the lack of an effective review mechanism to determine if cases have been improperly denied. Many problems might be corrected if an appellate mechanism, independent of the INS, existed to which those in the camps could appeal a written statement of findings and reasons. It is therefore advisable that a central review board be instituted at the Department of Justice to hear cases of appeals for rejected individuals. This would allow a separate review of individual grievances, and would systematize the process of appeal. Currently, INS officials have to cope with, and they complain about, a variety of pressures from those seeking reversals of prior determinations. The INS receives letters from Congress, as well as pressure from outside individuals and groups regarding specific cases, not to mention letters from those in the camp seeking re-presentation of their cases. Having an accepted appellate process would channel inquiries into one specific place, and would relieve some of the pressure from INS officers in Bangkok. It would also, more importantly, result in reconsideration of meritorious cases.

Although the Guidelines currently provide for an appeal to Washington for those cases falling into the Guideline categories, in

117

reality this review is perfunctory and results in few reversals. Many individuals claiming to have been former military and/or in re-education camps are rejected by the INS. In addition, interviews were conducted with persons falling into other recognized categories who had also been rejected, including: a Chinese family living at Na Pho who have an enthusiastic U.S. sponsor in Connecticut, a Catholic man from Vietnam who served in the Vietnamese army, and a Buddhist Monk now living at Phanat Nikhom. INS officers see only an applicant's file on appeal, without any necessary statement of the findings and reasons for an INS officer's decision. Under these conditions, the appellate file review can accomplish little. An independent review process, however, which reviews written findings and reasons, has much to recommend it.

In addition to these general concerns, three specific areas seem to pose unique problems that require further review:

Khao I Dang. Review of cases at Khao I Dang camp, on the Cambodian border, has posed persistent problems. In theory, this camp contains those persons deemed most likely to be resettled in third countries, though many of these individuals have subsequently been rejected by the INS and/or by other countries. Controversy revolves around whether valid refugee claims were improperly rejected by the INS in the past, in particular, based on improper findings of participation in Khmer Rouge persecution. In 1985, a computer survey was done of the Khao I Dang rejected cases, as well as a selected review of these cases. Since that time, there has been more discussion of whether further review is necessary, in particular following the decision to close Khao I Dang and return those rejected applicants to the border area.

In light of the controversy over these cases, a detailed review would seem appropriate following promulgation of revised processing guidelines on the persecution issue, and following the issuance of new country condition reports. Although this review process need not require re-interviews of applicants at the outset, such a possibility should not be precluded in the event supplemental information is desired.

Minors. There is concern that cases of unaccompanied minors are not treated fairly and neutrally, and therefore at a general impartial review of this area would be appropriate. In general, the U.S. has agreed to accept all minors who satisfy refugee criteria and who have links with this country. In addition, the U. S. has agreed to take half of the remaining minors with refugee status.

Specific U.S. guidelines for handling minors have varied through the years and various U.S. government cables have been issued to update the policy on minors. Clear guidance and criteria are needed and some training is necessary to assure that these guidelines are adhered to. For example, a December 21, 1987 State Department cable notes that fear of persecution of the parents may lead to refugee status for the minor: "if there is reason to believe that the parents wish their child to be outside the country of origin on grounds of well-founded fear of persecution, the child himself may be presumed to have such fear." This information should be contained in the Worldwide Guidelines; guidelines on implementing this policy are also necessary.

At Na Pho, for example, sentiments were expressed that minors had no hope of resettlement in the U.S. In some cases, the belief was that the INS was concerned about the "anchor effect" of having a minor admitted to the U.S., i.e., a minor in the U.S. might also result in the later admittance of parents, siblings, etc., on immigrant visas. This belief appeared prevalent despite a recent State Department cable, which notes that "the fact that a minor may become an anchor should not repeat not be considered in evaluating the merits of the persecution claim." In other cases, it was suggested that minors with close ties to the U.S., such as parents in the U.S., should themselves wait for an immigrant visa instead of seeking refugee status. In general, there are 156 unaccompanied minors at Na Pho. None have been accepted by the INS for resettlement and 65 have been rejected. Of those rejected, 24 have a "close link" to the U.S., i.e., a parent or sibling residing in the U.S. There should be clear guidelines to assure a neutral application of refugee and immigrant visa criteria.

LAWYERS COMMITTEE FOR HUMAN RIGHTS

STAFF

MICHAEL H. POSNER
Executive Director

ARTHUR C. HELTON
Director, Political Asylum Project

PATRICIA ARMSTRONG
1988 Project Coordinator

JOHN A. ASSADI
Staff Attorney

RAYMOND BROWN
Office Services

MARTHA L. DOGGETT
Human Rights Program

MARYAM ELAHI
Human Rights Internship Program

MIGDALIA GLORIA
Secretary

MITCHELL HARTMAN
Volunteer Projects
Coordinator

TERRY HUTCHINSON
Records Manager

MARIE JEANNOT
Executive Assistant

JULIE A. LYNCH
Legal Assistant

MAKAU MATUA
Staff Attorney

MARTHA R. MOFFETT
Staff Attorney

SANDRA MORENO
Staff Attorney

BINAIFER NOWROJEE
Human Rights Program

MARGARET NICHOLSON
Director of Operations

VIRGINIA PETERS
Executive Assistant

PAMELA PRICE
Coordinator, Lawyer-to-
Lawyer Project

JEMERA RONE
Central America
Representative (Part-time)

JAMES D. ROSS
Staff Attorney

VIRGINIA SHERRY
Director, Special Projects

WALTER WEISS
Staff Attorney

Since 1978, the Lawyers Committee for Human Rights has worked to protect and promote fundamental human rights around the world. The Committee has also been at the forefront of efforts to uphold the right of refugees, in flight from political persecution, to seek asylum in the United States.

The Committee has investigated human rights violations -- and broader patterns of systemic abuse -- in over 40 countries, including El Salvador, Nicaragua, Haiti, Poland, the Soviet Union, South Africa, Zimbabwe, Liberia, Pakistan, the Philippines and Cambodia. The Committee's work is non-partisan: each government -- regardless of its political orientation -- is held to the international standards affirmed in the Universal Declaration of Human Rights and codified in broadly accepted instruments of international law. The Committee works to promote the core group of rights that guarantee the integrity of the person:

* the right to be free from torture, summary execution, abduction or disappearance;

* the right to be free from arbitrary arrest, imprisonment without charge or trial, and indefinite incommunicado detention; and

* the right to due process and a fair trial before an independent judiciary.

IF YOU WOULD LIKE A COPY OF THE COMMITTEE'S 1988 ANNUAL REPORT -- WHICH DESCRIBES OUR WORK SINCE 1978 -- PLEASE WRITE TO US AT:

330 Seventh Avenue, New York, New York 10001